On
Loneliness

On Loneliness

How to Feel Less Alone
In an Isolating World

Terri Laxton Brooks

SHE WRITES PRESS

To Family and Friends
and to the memory of Kenny and Billy
whom we miss

To those suffering from loneliness
and loss in the time of COVID

"The secret of loneliness.
How to live with it, how to wrap it around your body
and still be able to make beautiful, colorful things..."

Excerpt from the novel *The Space Between Us*
by Thrity Umrigar

Contents

1

Personal Notes

"We are lonely. And in our blind reaching out,
we do not see how we embrace our own loneliness
and carry it with us, hugged against our chests."

(*Conversation with a friend*)

I asked a man to sleep with me last night. He was my friend—
affectionate, handsome, and, most important, available. After
I asked him, he sat very quietly on the footstool near my chair
for several minutes, and then he said no. I felt rejected, hurt, and
when he left, I asked myself why I needed affection and closeness
so desperately that I had to use sex to get it.*

I have felt this kind of loneliness all my life.

I grew up in a small town where everyone thought they knew
me, but no one knew me at all. During high school, I worked weekends in a coffee shop. While serving up the pecan pie, I would tell

---

* This book is based on my personal heterosexual experience and identity. I have also
drawn on or quoted psychologists and academics who assumed heterosexuality was
the only acceptable sexual orientation and gender identity, which was common for
the time. Those times have, thankfully, changed. But people's needs for personal happiness have not. When it comes to love and loneliness—no matter where a person
falls within the constellation of sexual orientation and gender identity—our basic
desires for loving, caring, bonding, and building a life together remain the same.

my customers that one day I would move to France. I dreamed of escape. My white uniform, black nylon apron with grease stains, white rubber-soled shoes—they were my prison uniform. The town, I thought, was my prison cell. My way of coping with the present was to ignore it. By the time I went to college, I was unable to relate to the people around me. I circled inward in ever-tighter knots and took in nothing that might infringe on my private world.

Then I married a man I'd known since I was sixteen. I married because I was under the illusion that a husband would end my loneliness. Some people have children for the same reason, and it is painful to learn that children or spouses are only a distraction from loneliness and not a cure. I imagined, as John Fowles says of his Victorian lovers in *French Lieutenant's Woman,* that my husband and I would lie for days in each other's arms in some jasmine-scented room, "infinitely alone, exiled, yet fused in that loneliness, inseparable in that exile." I married him not for what he was, but for what I wanted to become with him. I should have known better. But even after all these years, I still think, from time to time, that some man can save me.

I wanted to know how to love realistically, but I had no idea of where to begin. We need love, we need affection, and it is because of the misconceptions and fantasies we have about love, because of the distorted search and the broken dreams, that we sometimes cry out in our sleep.

When the marriage ended, I had to face a new and worse kind of loneliness. It pounced on me with all its might and simply would not let go. We were together always, sometimes at peace but more often at war. I took a lover and he turned off the lights during sex. I hoped he would remember who he was with. I hoped I would remember.

After sex, I turned away in bed. "You're awfully quiet," he said. "What are you thinking about?"

"It isn't important," I answered.

He persisted.

"I feel empty," I said, "because I just gave away too much of myself in bed." He was silent. And in that short night, I had somehow retrieved myself by hurting him with my words. I wondered how I would salvage the joy I knew was in life and how and where I would learn to ask for what I really needed.

Finally, I called a therapist. The first day I walked into the office, I saw a scrawled drawing tacked on the wall. I went over to it and smiled. It showed a child behind a table set up like a lemonade stand, but instead of lemonade a handwritten sign said: CURES FOR DAILY LONELINESS. $2.00

That was the loneliness I had come to have treated—not pathological loneliness but the common garden variety that comes upon us day by day. I sought a therapist's help because I was living alone, had recently moved, and had few friends. A love affair had ended.

I felt afraid. Over the years, my friends have changed. People who once plunged into life now feared it, people who once had dreams settled for security. So many people chose to be safe rather than run the risk of being alone and lonely. Their lives seemed sterile, barren, frightening. Now I felt it was happening to me.

I wanted to flee to safety and had nowhere to run; I had given myself too much freedom and couldn't stand the pain. My sense of isolation from myself and others threatened to engulf me. It became crucial to me to understand what was going on—the source of and the force behind this loneliness that touches me and the people close to me.

I once wondered who among us is lonely. Now it seems that the answer is: we all are at some time. People who say that they are never lonely are simply not in touch with their feelings, or unwilling to give in to them.

On Loneliness

"The problem with loneliness," a friend told me, "is that we treat it like a skinned knee." I understood what he meant. We treat loneliness like an unexpected and unimportant pain. It is a transient condition, one that will heal by tomorrow. It is the result of some misstep in our lives. We act as if it were a price we pay for being careless in our relationships. We can understand loneliness in the hospital, loneliness on a business trip, even loneliness in a crowd. But it is the one thing in life we do not expect when everything is going right.

"Loneliness is a gruesome topic," my friend went on. "It's like going into the lion's den and saying: 'Are you hungry, lion?' It'll be painful to write about," he warned, "with people slobbering over their deepest and most secret feelings." Yes, I thought, perhaps he is right. But I didn't know the half of it.

After I began this book, I asked a noted psychiatrist I knew if he were ever lonely. "Yes," he said. "How do you handle it?" I asked. "I read in bed and drink wine until I fall asleep," he said. I found his reaction is not uncommon. He could help other people deal with their loneliness but couldn't deal with his own. It has disturbed me to discover how many of the people who are supposed to know about our emotions often don't understand loneliness—their own or anybody else's. They have a hands-off, antiseptic attitude. They talk about the loneliness of the aged, of widows, of the institutionalized, but seldom of their own experience. The effect of loneliness in their lives and ours has been completely ignored, as the dynamics of death and dying were ignored until only a few years ago.

When I talked to people about writing this book, many of them would say: "I'd love to talk to you about it sometime—I know *all* about loneliness. Let's meet for drinks some night." And I'd never hear from them again. Others made slighting, often uneasy remarks about my preoccupation with loneliness. There was almost a social stigma attached to mentioning it. I felt they were wondering why I spent time thinking and writing about a subject "healthy" people avoid. I began to feel, when asked what I was writing about, that when I said "loneliness" the word should be followed by a catch in my voice, a batted eyelash . . . they expected more of me once I dropped that leaden word.

William Sadler, Jr., a professor of sociology, taught a course on loneliness at Bloomfield College in New Jersey and said his students were often embarrassed about taking the subject: "It's like holding a class on alcoholism or homosexuality—as if attending would be to declare themselves," he said. "But in my class, they learned it's okay to admit loneliness. It's like saying: 'I'm tired, or I'm horny, or I'm anxious.'"

Perhaps the reason there have been so few studies on loneliness is that we are ashamed to admit our familiarity with it—as if we have made an embarrassing pact with the devil. We talk about our sex lives in public, even the condition of our bowels, but when did you last hear anyone at a cocktail party discuss their loneliness?

"My father, when I was growing up, didn't say: 'Prepare for loneliness. You're going to be lonely when you're older,'" Sadler told me. "What he said was: 'Develop a personality so you will be popular, be liked, be successful, and if you work hard at that, you will be a happy man.' So when my own loneliness came I said to myself: 'What's wrong with me? What's happening?' It didn't conform with my expectations. I didn't believe it. I rejected it, dismissed it. The confusion, the resistance to it, made my loneliness even worse."

I suppose these attitudes are why there has been so little serious examination of loneliness in the average person. This is why I began this book—out of frustration at finding so little to give my own experience some shape, some meaning.

On Loneliness

This book is about the ordinary lonelinesss felt by most people, a feeling that is all the more unbearable because it often has no obvious cause and seems so inescapable. We go to therapists for depression, anxiety, or fear but seldom for just plain loneliness. But one thing each depressed person, each anxious person, each fearful person has in common is this: the feeling of being unconnected, unwhole, misunderstood. These feelings are all a part of being lonely.

This book is about lovers, husbands, children, mothers, fathers—people regardless of where they fall on the spectrum of gender identity and sexual preference—who can speak thoughtfully and without fear about their loneliness.

This book is about people I know well and people I barely know at all, people I met by appointment in offices, by chance in bars, and on the street. It is about loneliness on a country porch and a city stoop. It is about the difference between aloneness and loneliness, about the different faces of loneliness, and why some people are better able to handle it than others. It is about the nighttime cry of an unloved child, the morning cry of an abandoned lover.

It is about the analyst's couch, which has left us staring with bitterness and pain across the chasm of our childhoods at the specter of our parents and has left parents behind, left them out, wondering what went wrong.

This is a book about the splintering of lives into meaningless pieces, about the fault lines of our lives. It is about people who are restless when alone in the country, about how busywork becomes a narcotic. It is a book about why people suffer and hurt. It is about how our longing for love and companionship frightens and confuses us and makes us say yes when we really mean no, how the emptiness and restlessness we feel in our early years can follow us through middle age and on to death.

This book is about why loneliness drives some people crazy and makes some people strong. Why the fear of it makes some people dependent, stay in bad marriages and unhealthy relationships. It is about why people are afraid to be intimate.

This book includes some philosophy, some psychology, and many examples of other people's loneliness. And it will give you some insights into how to handle your own. But mainly, inevitably, it is a personal book, and my written words a sort of coarse sieve between what people tell me and what I tell you. Because it is a personal book, I do not write specifically of loneliness as a medical or psychological problem. I do not write about the problems of aging and loneliness, or loneliness in institutions such as hospitals or nursing homes. I deal with average middle-class loneliness—the kind I have become familiar with in my day-to-day and year-by-year experience.

I have lived with loneliness for much longer than I have acknowledged it, and often chose to ignore it rather than face it. Much of what I put down here is rumination, like moving a picture from wall to wall, up and down, eyeing it, testing it to see where it fits best.

This is what I wonder about loneliness: If we can identify the way it is disguised in our deepest emotions and needs, then perhaps we can begin to better understand why it exists and what we should do about it—assuming that what we are now doing isn't good enough and assuming that it is in our best interests to do anything about it at all.

For one thing I have learned is that loneliness does not have to be destructive. In fact, it can be quite the opposite: positive, invigorating, fortifying, like a dive into cold water on a sultry day. But in order for us to know whether it will harm us or help us, we must first be able to recognize its face, be aware when it strikes, understand why, and know what it does to our lives. All people are lonely some of the time, but most people are lonely too much of the time.

2

The Nature
of Loneliness

"This is the universal human condition: There is a void
at the center of every psyche. You can call it the absent mother . . .
divine restlessness, or the unreasonable fear of death.
But it seems to be characteristic of every person."

(Sam Keen, "A Conversation with Oscar Ichazo," Psychology Today)

One bright sunny morning I woke up in a hotel room in San Diego, turned over in the queen-sized bed, looked at the ocean waves lapping beyond the window, and realized that here, in this idyllic setting, I was lonely. I had been traveling alone and slept one too many nights by myself in hotel rooms, eaten one too many meals alone in restaurants. Loneliness had struck, no doubt about it, and it was awful. I changed my travel plans and flew home that day.

Yet, that is not the only kind of loneliness I feel, nor is it always so easily resolved. There are many other kinds, more subtle and unexpected.

Recently, I was sitting alone in the backyard of a friend's house. The moon was a sliver of light. There were no stars. I heard crickets and the rummaging of a raccoon. Fireflies winked—flashing arcs in the bushes ahead of me. The grass breathed chill and damp under my feet. It was silent. I sensed my body dying, cell by cell, there in the dark. I realized that when I left this bench it would be as if I had never been there. The grass would spring back where my feet had rested. I would leave behind no trace. I heard a telephone ringing in a distant house, and suddenly I wanted to go inside and call someone, anyone.

I felt transient, insignificant, and the sense of my separateness filled me with a deep, flowing loneliness. Yet I sat quietly a moment longer, for I also sensed my uniqueness. I felt reflective and calm. All my life I have surrounded myself with things and people. But I realized that reality is here, in the stillness of this summer night. Each person is ultimately alone. In my life, I take on no passengers and have no baggage. No one else can breathe for me, or speak for me. I die alone.

Here, then, were two completely different kinds of loneliness—with different causes and effects on me. In fact, the feelings provoked were so varied that it seems strange to attach just one word to both of them.

I suspect one reason we have trouble recognizing and handling our loneliness is for this very reason—because we tend to suppress and transform emotions, especially negative ones like fear, anger, and loneliness. It is easy for us to talk about objects in our lives, but we run into trouble when we try to articulate feelings.

The result is that although we feel many kinds of loneliness, we have only one word to describe them all. The same is true of love: There are many ways of loving, but only one word to encompass them all, and we are reduced to using mechanistic words like "relationship." To describe loneliness accurately, most people have to begin by describing the situation that makes them feel lonely, and go from there.

The Nature of Loneliness

Loneliness can be triggered by something internal, from inside our heads, or by something external from people we are near or situations we are in. People who feel unloved as children often feel this internal loneliness; they may have spouses or lovers and still feel that the love they are sharing is not real or deserved.

Harry Guntrip, a psychotherapist at Leeds University in England, found among his patients that: "The love-starved child who is terrified of being alone is fighting for what is after all his elementary right to the primary supportive relationship that can alone enable him to live. If he had had it at the right time in infancy, he would not now be so cruelly undermined and dependent on other people." People who do not get the love they need as children spend the rest of their lives looking for someone to make it up to them.

A friend of mine, for instance, who has always described his mother as a "cold bitch," and whose father died when he was young, married in a desperate effort to ward off a lifetime of depression and loneliness. "I thought I was saving myself," he said. "But after the wedding, I still didn't feel loved, and I didn't know how to love." His sense of isolation continued to haunt him, and so the marriage failed. Regardless of the living situation, the adult who was an unloved child often cannot give and receive love as easily as other people can.

This internal loneliness can also be a reaction to other insecurities and unfilled needs that have dogged us through the years. This is the source of much of the loneliness I feel. As an adolescent, everybody feels different and misunderstood. But I didn't grow out of it. I perpetuated this feeling and shut myself off from people. I disguised my sense of inadequacy by smiling or retreating into hostile silence. I avoided people because it seemed to me they forced me to play a role I didn't want to play. In short, I, like many other people, did not grow up—my emotions remained adolescent.

On Loneliness

There is another kind of loneliness, caused by an experience or a situation, which is much easier to deal with. A guidance counselor told me of the loneliness that haunts her whenever she goes into her supermarket. "That's where you meet all the lonely people; they talk to you in line. You look in their grocery cart and you see they bought half a loaf of bread, half a dozen eggs, one small yogurt, one tomato. It's a dead giveaway. Someday I will probably live alone and go through that. People will look at my meager purchases and think: 'Oh, that poor old lady; she lives alone.' I would rather buy a lot of food and throw half of it away than expose myself to that sort of pity."

Another woman I know feels most lonely in the subway during rush hour, when people are crushed up against her. "It's awful," she says, "because the people who are touching me don't know or care who I am or how I feel."

Some feel loneliest with their families, or during Christmas holidays—at the times when they should feel warm and good but, instead, feel isolated, feel that they and their families don't really have much in common. This comes as a shock. We have all been taught that these moments of togetherness should be the ones that make us feel we belong. At a party one evening, a biologist told me that when he was growing up, he identified love with food. "At mealtime, the whole family would try to act close, but would always end up bickering," he said. "I kept trying through those meals to live up to the dream, and the only result was that I got fat. But I still feel the urge to go home for all the holidays. I'm still searching for that promised dinner that will represent warmth and unity."

When a marriage ends by mutual consent, both spouses seem to be afflicted by post-marital emptiness. The routines they have grown accustomed to no longer exist. The resentment, bitterness, and hatreds that once consumed so much time and energy are now meaningless and leave an emotional void.

The Nature of Loneliness

We feel yet a different kind of loneliness when we break up with a lover, or say goodbye to a friend we won't see for a long time, or when we move. It can end as abruptly as it began once we find a new lover, a good friend, or cordial neighbors. Robert Weiss, a former psychiatrist at Harvard Medical School, said that then "loneliness will vanish abruptly and without a trace, as though it never had existed. There is no gradual recovery, no getting over it bit by bit. When it ends, it ends suddenly; one was lonely, one is not anymore."

It was helpful to me when William Sadler, Jr. divided loneliness into categories: Interpersonal—when you miss someone you love; Social—when you are excluded from a group; Cultural—when you feel cut off from a tradition, from familiar values and roots (the loneliness of immigrants and travelers); Cosmic—when you feel the universe is absurd, life is pointless, God is lost (the loneliness of the existentialist); and Psychological—when you feel alienated from yourself and out of touch with your true nature.

"In each case," said Sadler, "the person perceives himself to be cut off from another person, from himself, a group, a tradition, a universe, a god. So when the person says, 'I feel lonely,' well, you have to ask: 'Where do you feel lonely?' If the person feels loved by friends and family but also feels the world is falling apart, that he can't hook in, that he feels uprooted and meaningless, then that's a special kind of loneliness, and you can't solve it by having someone come in and hold his hand."

We who live in Western countries probably feel this "world-is-falling-apart" loneliness more often and for more reasons than people ever have before. I will discuss this more in Chapter Nine, but I want to point out here that one source of our loneliness is our tarnished sense of pride in our work, our country, and our politics. All these continue to deteriorate. So far, nothing has come to take their place. At the same time, we have higher expectations for a fulfilling life but fewer ways to reach our goals. All this makes us feel unfocused, frustrated, and empty inside.

Those who worry about getting enough rice to eat don't have time to worry about boredom and inner emptiness. But those of us who have enough rice now want the rice to be "meaningful." First, we want warm clothes, and then we want them tailor-made. When our dreams come true we feel a certain vacuum inside because we no longer have a goal. We search for new dreams, and the searching leaves us with a constant sense of loss, and fills us with a vague longing, nostalgia, and discontent.

These feelings are the ones we often distort or push away. We give a party, or go to one, and feel better for a while. Then the feeling creeps up and surprises us again. It invades us even on our sunny days. When we least expect it, when everything is going right, we sense it just behind us, ready to pounce.

We sometimes assume that being lonely and being alone are the same thing. But this is not the case. There are people who are never alone and still feel lonely. Someone who spends afternoons in the office with clients and evenings with family; a stay-at-home parent busy twenty-four hours a day with the children and shopping and cooking, often yearns for time to be alone. If you ask these people if they're lonely, they often look at you in astonishment or amusement and say: "I don't have time to be lonely." But, in fact, many people, hemmed in by these situations, do feel alienated from themselves; they have a sense of being incomplete and dissatisfied and feel a restless urge to "get away." This is loneliness in one of its forms. This is the loneliness of the person who never has time to sit quietly, reflect, and enjoy their own company.

There is a difference between loneliness and aloneness. You feel comfortable when you are simply alone. You *choose* to be alone. When you are isolated from other people and still feel whole, when you feel at ease with yourself, centered, then you are simply alone. As Walt Whitman described it: "I exist as I am, that is enough/ If no other in the world be aware/ I sit content/ And if each and all be aware/ I sit content."

Loneliness, on the other hand, includes a feeling of discontent and rejection. It is a sense of being helpless, trapped in a physical or emotional limbo. It comes when you feel threatened by being alone, when you feel something is missing. It is a desire for something outside yourself: You believe another person, another place can make you feel happier than you feel now.

Perhaps we confuse being alone with being lonely because both are considered un-American activities. We frown on people who spend a lot of time alone: We call them antisocial or loners. At home, we discipline children by sending them to their rooms, and in school we banish them from the classroom or sequester them in corners. This is the message: To be alone is rejection. When we are put in these situations we are told we are unacceptable, cast away from our peers, inferior, different. We are taught that aloneness is a form of punishment.

Advertising harps on the stigma of being alone. "Normal" people should be in pairs or groups, not by themselves while everyone else is having fun.

Ads imply that people are alone—especially young people—because they aren't attractive enough, cool enough, have bad hair days, flabby abs, wear the wrong clothes, have the wrong body shape, or aren't cheerful enough—and in that case, pop a happy pill and friends will flock to you. The subliminal message is that no one wants to be alone by choice. We like to believe we don't fall for advertisers' claims. But a psychologist told me that many of the clients he sees avoid close relationships because they believe they have these kinds of imperfections that lead to ridicule or shaming.

On Loneliness

Traditionally, the important events of our lives are shared. Team spirit is part of our heritage. We moved West in caravans, had barn-raisings to help settle new families. We remain joiners to this day. Group rates, package tours, and private clubs are an important part of the American culture.

But all this togetherness isn't always good for us. Any animal crowded in a cage with no private space becomes frantic, irritated, and often develops emotional problems. Humans, too, require a certain amount of isolation. A psychologist told me that the loneliest people she sees are the ones who have no privacy. We know this instinctively, and we find ways to get off by ourselves. We develop colds or stomachaches when unwanted visitors arrive, or when we have to go somewhere we don't want to, and the symptoms seem to just disappear when we are left alone. I suspect we love our automobiles for more than just mobility and convenience. We will continue to drive them, no matter how big the traffic jams, how polluting the car, or how expensive the gas, because they give us a chance to be alone, and to be in control.

I know a woman—a wife, mother, and full-time professor—whose idea of heaven is to come home to an empty house. On those those rare occasions, she says, she feels wonderful when she can read in peace and eat alone. Her occasional business trips are also a refuge. "I love checking into a hotel where no one knows me," she says. "I have food sent up, I sink into a hot tub, and I read half the night."

The ability to be alone without feeling lonely varies from person to person. I have a friend who lives alone in a house in the country and she is seldom lonely. I have another friend who lives in New York City and is busy every night and she is often lonely.

I find the country friend to be more interesting. She feels better about herself, values herself independently of things and people around her, and does not need to turn on the television the minute she is by herself. The city friend, on the other hand, gets bored if she is home before midnight. These two people differ in their psychological makeup, how they were brought up, and how they approach life. All of this is reflected in their ability to be alone without feeling threatened.

Their environments also influence them. The country friend is accustomed to a quieter life; the city friend is used to action. Dr. Frank Mark, a former special assistant at the Department of Health, Education, and Welfare in Washington, said: "We get programmed to have a certain number of contact points through each day, either with other people or through the media. If you increase or decrease the input, it will lead to a certain amount of loneliness. It depends on how much you are used to taking in. If I come home at night and my wife is out and the kids are gone, I get very lonely because these people mean a lot to me and I am used to having them around. If they were never around, I eventually wouldn't miss them as much."

Because I am used to spending a lot of time alone, I can be home by myself all day and not feel lonely as long as a few friends phone me or I make some plans for the evening or my work is going well. I also find that my loneliness is cyclical. What bothers me today may not bother me tomorrow. A chance encounter in the street, a break from my normal routine, can change my entire outlook and give me the feeling that things aren't as bad as they seemed an hour ago. Sometimes my mood improves when I talk to people, take a long slow walk, or go to a movie. Sometimes if I just sit with the loneliness a while, without distracting myself with busy work, I find it goes away of its own accord.

3

Childhood

"I would that life should hurt you, and you be unafraid of pain."
(East Indian mother's poem to her child)

Two children I know play a favorite weekend game in which
they rise at dawn to unwind spools of black thread in a long
continuous web around all sleeping adults in the house—around
bedposts, through hallways, under chairs, and over arms and legs.
When we awake, the invisible web snares us again and again as
we make our way stumbling and laughing from bed to kitchen. I
have come to think of these tangled morning webs as my own, the
dark morning memories of childhood, the shadowed ones that
silently and unexpectedly trip me up as I move in measured paces
through my home and through my day.

Each of us carries a child within. That child is the acorn that
contains the oak and feeds every fiber of the growing tree. The
loneliness we feel today comes from a loneliness we felt before
when we were young, even at birth. There is no escaping it, and
perhaps we should not try.

Loneliness is a pain that is intrinsic to life. We all feel the anxiety of loss from the time we are born. We react differently to it

because we are different. Each of us is unique. Even during birth, each newborn infant acts and moves differently as it comes from the womb. Some kick more fiercely, some are more restless, some pucker, and others frown.

As we grow, we learn to adapt to our loneliness. We develop patterns to handle in a safe way the fears that we feel in life. At some point, we make a subconscious decision about how we are going to deal with the anxiety that loneliness brings. As adults, we too often forget that the way we handle exclusion, isolation, or ostracism largely depends on how we learned to handle these crises in our youth. We forget that our first, early responses to loneliness and loss follow us until the day we die.

When I was seven years old, I frightened my baby brother and he fell headfirst through a window. We were playing hide-and-seek, and he was perched on the back of the living room couch looking for me. Behind him was a large bay window. I jumped out from my hiding place, he lost his balance and fell backward, crashing through the window and landing on the front porch. My mother came running, wrapped a towel around his bloody head, and hailed a passing car, which raced them to the hospital. I was sure I had killed him. I ran to my room and hid.

Now my brother has just a thin scar to remind us of that day, but the memory of it sticks like a cracker in a dry throat, for I was lonely, burdened with my guilt, isolated in my shame, and certain I would be cast out by my family.

There were other times of loneliness and terror. And it is curious how I cling to them. If I made a list of events from ages one to seventeen and tallied up the bad memories in one column and the good memories in the other, I would probably end up with a mathematically "happy" childhood. But, in fact, if you give a child a piece of candy and ask, "Are you happy?" the child will likely answer "Yes," and if you tell her ten minutes later that she must go to bed rather than play, and then ask her if she is happy, she will answer "No," for happiness in a child's world is as reliable as the weather in Chicago. Even though a child may appear relaxed and happy, much is buried underneath, embroiled in a world of fantasies and fears. A secret and very lonely world.

A friend told me that the first time her parents left her alone, she became hysterical. Her mother and father were only going to a house a few doors away, but she did all she could to make them stay. She screamed and vomited on the living room couch. But they left just the same, and when they returned a few hours later, she was face down on the floor, still sobbing, still convinced beyond reason that they would never return. It was, she says, the first time she understood that each time you expose yourself to love, you must prepare yourself for loneliness. She tells me about it now because her lover has just left her, and her face tenses in the old encrusted pain.

St. Paul said: "When I was a child I spake as a child, I understood as a child, I thought as a child; but when I became a man, I put away childish thngs." But it is not that simple. We don't throw away our childish things. We hoard them in an attic.

I once saw a cartoon in which a child about to cry was carrying on a monologue about his fears: Fear of going to school because his parents might move without telling him; fear of falling asleep because a boogeyman might get him; fear of going out to play because his parents might not hear him at the door to let him back in.

This is the lonely reality of childhood, and anyone who insists they had a perfectly unflawed and happy childhood more likely has a faulty memory.

We must know (in the instinctive, not the intellectual, sense of "knowing") from the instant we leave the womb what it is like to be lonely, to be separated from comfort and security. "In the womb, there is no gap between desire and satisfaction. We sense the change as separation and loss, as abandonment, as a fall into a strange or hostile atmosphere," Octavio Paz suggested in *The Labyrinth of Solitude.* I wonder how he knows. I suspect he is right. In the womb we are one with our mother who is the world. We do not have to wait for our food; it is there and we are never hungry. We do not have trouble sleeping; a liquid cushion protects us from the world. We do not want what we cannot have; so we have everything we want. We are not social, not concerned with love and hate, lust and shame, or any of the things that worry us in the world. We simply are. And then we are born. We are pushed from the womb.

It must be a shock to find we are encased in our own skins. It must be a shock to enter the world, and the loss of the womb is our first great loss. Psychoanalyst Otto Rank said that birth trauma is the "most painful of all memories" and that some types of phobias (like claustrophobia, or fear of tunnels) are just a replay of the anxiety we felt when coming down the birth canal. "The child's constant proneness to anxiety," Rank said, "originates in the birth trauma and is transferable to almost anything."

I close my eyes and try to recall my womb-world, but I come up with only the suffused red tones of the membranes behind my eyelids. The rest is lost, completely and irrevocably, and it makes me realize to what extent I am a prisoner of my mind, trapped by those forgotten fears that are recorded in the centers of my brain.

We must recall at some level what it is like to fall from Paradise to something a little less than Paradise, and a lot of us waste time trying to go back. We must recall the panic and anger of suddenly being separate and alone, and some of us still have a hard time getting used to it fifty years later, and some of us never do.

It is only in the last few decades that tenderness and human contact has become a priority for American hospitals welcoming healthy babies. Hospitals now encourage moms to breastfeed, help them start doing so within an hour after birth, and let their baby room-in during the hospital stay. In the past, babies arrived under harsh lights, were isolated in bassinettes, fed on a schedule other than their own, and, if taken to the mother's breast, not left there long enough for intimacy.

French gynecologist Frederick Leboyer said most babies reacted violently to those standard delivery room conditions. "That tragic expression, those tight-shut eyes, that howling mouth . . . pictures of newborn infants could equally well be pictures of criminals who have undergone torture and are about to die," Leboyer said, "as if our deliberate intention was to teach the child that it had fallen into a world of ignorance, cruelty, and folly." Leboyer believed these birth techniques heightened a child's feeling of being alone and threatened by the surrounding world.

Some of our feelings of loss also come from weaning. Our mouth is our first erogenous zone and the breast we suck gives us pleasure as well as food. Weaning from the breast, especially when done abruptly, can produce acute depression in the child and even chronic states of mourning, said developmental psychologist Erik Erikson, which can "give a depressive undertone to the remainder of one's life."

When our mouth, our source of pleasure, becomes a source of pain during teething, we discover for the first time the full force of masochistic "evil" in the world. And when we do, our howls may well include some outrage and anger as well as pain.

Any early separation from the mother seems to have a profound and lasting effect. Harry Guntrip noted that children who are left alone in hospitals at first cry and look for their mothers but eventually give up, become listless and depressed. When they begin to play again, they are indifferent to which nurses take care of them. When these children see their parents again, many do not recognize their mothers, only their fathers, which means they did not forget their mothers—they just didn't forgive them. Guntrip says that these phases of protest, despair, and detachment are remarkably similar to the mourning that adults go through when a friend or a close relative dies.

We get back at our parents in small ways. I remember gathering all my toys in a corner when friends would come over to play, and then refusing to let anyone near them, knowing this tactic would upset my mother and get me her full and undivided attention. Some children get their revenge on the toilet, for toilet training is a major parental concern. To get attention, all you have to do is wet the bed.

Some of our childhood games are played in deadly earnest. The guerrilla warfare that sometimes seems to escalate in the nursery, the small cruelties children inflict on one another, teasing and poking, hair-pulling and shoving, just might be a reflection of how they perceive themselves being treated—or mistreated—by adults.

Play is one of our earliest ways of releasing aggression, and people who do not learn how to play are often potentially dangerous adults. If we learn the right games in childhood, they help us as adults, and if we learn the wrong games, or learn the games wrongly, they can destroy us. We wrestle when we are younger and slam each other around the football field when we are older, and they are rooted in the same needs we had when we were two.

In twenty-five years of practice, Guntrip found that all forms of aggression are reactions to our basic fears of isolation. Ernest Becker, author of *Denial of Death*, takes this one step further and says all our aggressions, need to be heroic, our drive to win—as reflected, in this case, in games—are mechanisms we use to stave off our fear of the ultimate loneliness: death.

Games are our earliest form of communication. If we cannot

communicate as children, we will have a difficult time learning to communicate as adults. The inability to play can breed a lifelong cycle of isolation and loneliness. This is why children's games are sometimes used in psychotherapy. They teach adults things they should have learned as children. There is a marriage counseling technique, for example, in which spouses sit back to back on the floor with Tinkertoys. One builds something with the Tinkertoys and describes each piece as it is put together, and the other has to build the same structure by following the partner's verbal directions without asking questions. People who play this game often find out about their communication patterns and discover that they have forgotten how to communicate well.

In our infantile hours of loss and loneliness, we bounce on beds and bang our toys to relieve our frustration. We sleep in closets and suck our thumbs or latch onto favorite dolls to feel safe and secure. I had a security blanket which my mother weaned me from by periodically cutting it in half with her sewing shears until it was reduced to a small rag, which I lost without much grief. But I replaced it with other props. I learned early on that a book in front of my face was a perfect escape from the confusing (to me) drama of my family. Later I escaped into journalism, replacing the book with a typewriter and then ever-faster computers on which I wrote stories about other people's lives to avoid dealing with my own

We act out our fears until we are eventually told to stop "acting childish." And because we want to please and to be accepted, we learn instead to act "like an adult," which means that instead of banging our toys we honk our horns in traffic, and instead of sucking our thumbs we overeat, and we wonder why we still feel frustrated and lonely. But we never forget the times we first felt deserted and alone. These insidious memories stamp patterns of behavior and response into our brains so that far too often we wander mindlessly around life like French entomologist J. Henri Fabre's caterpillars, which endlessly circled the rim of a vase, blindly following old silken tracks laid down long ago that never led them anywhere.

We depend on our parents' love to make us feel secure and wanted, and our parents are bound to disappoint us. Many parents are often, for all practical purposes, absent even when they are physically present. They may be distracted by domestic chores, juggling work and home, wrapped up in their own frustration and boredom, worries and fears. No matter how wonderful parents are, they cannot live up to, or even know, our expectations all the time. We feel unjustly punished, unexplainably ignored, and left alone. We are sent to bed early while the adults stay up; we are not always permitted to go outside to play with friends; we must eat when we aren't hungry. One or both of our parents leave without us for a vacation—or leave entirely—and we are suddenly thrown into a desolate, strange, and alien world.

And we relive the feelings of that world each time a lover leaves us, a friend dies or moves away, a promotion falls through, a neighbor is robbed, a child is sick.

Not all our childhood memories are of loneliness. There are moments of applause: the wrestling trophy, the Girl Scout badge. We still have those too, and if you are like me, you have the documents and photos stashed in a cardboard box where they wait to be discovered by your children or rediscovered by the child in you.

But those other not-so-pleasant memories are the ones that stick, and we do not keep them in cardboard boxes. Those crises and disappointments, the sense of not belonging, of not being loved or lovable, not being good enough, tall enough, smart enough, funny enough, those little chunks of loneliness—those we shove in the corner of our minds hoping to forget them. But we find when the time comes (and for thinking, sensitive adults the time does come) that we never really forgot about those things at all.

Why do they haunt us?

A therapist explained to me that all our feelings of intimacy and rejection are developed in the first years of life. We all need lots of mother love: Even a monkey will grow up neurotic, frightened, and unable to reproduce if it isn't cuddled in its early months. "The first [affectionate] bond and usually the most persistent of all is that between mother and young," wrote psychoanalyst John Bowlby. "[It] sets a pattern which deeply influences the way that, subsequently, his or her sexual behavior and caretaking behavior become organized . . . in humans, attachment behavior is probably at its most striking during the second and third year of life . . . it is a normal and healthy part of human nature from the cradle to the grave."

I know a young man, a medical student, who has trouble feeling. Instead, he intellectualizes everything. When he was a baby he had polio and spent most of his childhood in hospitals. Doctors and nurses lavished care on him, but having consistent close physical contact with his mother was impossible. When he was finally home with his family, he felt emotionally numb. "I was nine when my parents sent me to a therapist. I did play therapy. I used to make clay people and then cut them up, doing to them what the world had done to me," he says. The world still seems a confusing, menacing place to him.

"Why can a child explore the world endlessly?" he asks. "What allows him to do that? Why have we no longer that ability to explore an empty drawer? It's really not empty for a child; it's filled with dreams and desires. Children explore, with fingers in the mouth, with all parts of the body, the delight of feeling the world. We grow up and can't do that anymore." I watched him one day when a kitten jumped onto the couch where he was sitting and brushed against his thigh, purring. He likes cats but he did not spontaneously reach out and pet this kitten, as most other people would do. I saw his hand lift slightly and then fall back to his lap. He watched the animal without expression, unable to display even this simple affection.

There are healthy and unhealthy kinds of parental love. Some parents don't love their children at all, although they always say they do, and the child usually finds out the truth very soon. These children feel depressed and lonely most of their lives. Some parents love their children frantically, with a love so possessive and smothering that the children have a hard time finding themselves under the layers. Some parents love their children because they need to see their reflections in someone else. These children often go through life feeling they are loved for what they do or who they are *with* rather than for who they are. Too much of the wrong kind of love has, in the end, the same effect as no love at all. The child becomes detached, their emotions blocked or misdirected, and a new and very lonely person struggles to live in the world.

Parents are rarely intentionally cruel. Often they are just imitating the way they were brought up. Thirty years later, they are making the same mistakes with their own children that their parents made with them. When parents feel frustrated and unloved, children often become their innocent victims simply because they are there. As Philip Slater said in *Earthwalk,* "The unloved cannot love, and spread the disease to their children."

I know a woman who was so destroyed by her family life that she became a nun. Her father was an alcoholic; her parents fought all the time. She was taught that sex was a necessary evil. By the time she was a teenager, she realized she did not know anything about loving. She found the security and attention she needed in the convent. She left the convent when she felt mature and able to love. Now she is thinking about marrying and having children. One day over coffee she told me with a smile that she has her own definition of original sin: It is the passing of human hang-ups from generation to generation. Redemption, she said, is the freeing of ourselves from those tentacles of fear that pass for love.

Parents who know how to handle their anxieties, who don't feel threatened by other people or alienated from themselves, are free to love their children best. But there is probably not a single healthy child born who does not at some point feel the need to stand apart from even the best of parents to find oneself. Few parents or children are spared the agony of this separation, and it leads to a painful but healthy kind of loneliness.

Some parents cling long after their children are grown. One woman told me that when she moved to New York her mother sent her a box of clothing that was suitable for a teenager but not for a woman. When this woman was in graduate school, she still felt as if her mother were going to read her report card, as she had in high school. "She was nine hundred miles away," she says, "but if you grow up believing your parents can read your mind, they can read your mind wherever you are. You don't have to be in the same room.

"It took me a long time to give up the feeling of being totally dependent on my mother. I feared being alone. It terrified me. I didn't want to look at the fact that we are, every one of us, alone. I had to find a way to cut myself off from my mother and overcome the guilt about doing it. When I finally did it, I felt she was going to die or I was going to die. It gave me this terrible sense of my total aloneness."

When her own daughter was learning to talk, this woman stood with her in front of a full-length mirror and played a game.

On Loneliness

She would say: "Katie's eyes" and point to her daughter's eyes, and "Mommy's eyes" and point to her own; "Katie's nose, Mommy's nose," pointing to each. "No matter how much I love my daughter, if she cuts her finger, *her* finger bleeds, not mine. I can't bleed for her. In the mirror game and others, I taught her that we were similar but separate. It has caused me a lot of pain. We always want to hang onto our children. But it took my own pain of breaking from my mother to make me want to do that for her."

Some parents hold onto their children by hatred rather than love. They will deliberately do things to bait their children, knowing it will get a rise out of them. Or they will do things to worry their children, such as threaten suicide. This is another way of controlling children and preventing them from living an independent life. No matter how dependency between parents and children is disguised, the separation process is crucial. If your parent disapproves of your career or lifestyle, it is often because the mold they shaped for you is being broken. It is important for you to recognize the signs of an unhealthy symbiosis. You will have to find a way to free yourself or for the rest of your life you will circle around your parents like a satellite around a planet.

Breaking away is a ritual of growth. It took me until the age of thirty-five to be able to do it, and it was the most difficult step of my life. It took me all that time to figure out that the truth, as my mother sees it, is not my truth. And my truth, no matter how dearly won, will not set my child free. Because it is so hard to break away, many adults find themselves coming of age when they are forty or fifty. Years have little to do with it.

Octavio Paz says that every life that is truly autonomous begins "as a break with its family and its past. But the separation still hurts ... that is why the feeling of orphanhood is the constant background of our personal conflicts." I have found this to be the case. People who say they have never been lonely usually aren't very independent either.

This fear of loss is one reason why children do not move far from home and do not travel. The inability to separate is epitomized in the classic 1949 Arthur Miller play *Death of a Salesman* (which streams on several channels). Willy Loman, the salesman—full of fears and dreams and trapped in his past—never finds his way forward and saddles his sons with the same failed dreams. Although he has friends and a wife who loves him, his is the face of loneliness.

Because growth and separation are so difficult, some choose to live in totalitarian regimes rather than seek freedom, and others in democracies choose to conform. Some people never make the break. I know a woman whose father died unexpectedly. They had been very close. After his death, she went home and screamed at her lover that he too must leave because she couldn't bear it if he abandoned her later on. It is irrational, childish, and basic.

I know—or think I know—what the "ideal" family is, but I have seldom seen one. Last summer I was in the Albany airport waiting to take a plane to New York City and saw a family scene that reminded me of what I thought I'd missed. A middle-aged couple and their three children were waiting to greet their white-haired grandmother. The children were eager and laughing, the parents were talking to one another and smiling. When the grandmother arrived, there was much hugging and kissing and warmth between the three generations. The surface of their life looked smooth, unruffled, and serene. But I know it is seldom the way it seems.

I recently showed a friend a picture that was taken several years ago of my brothers, and then I described each brother one by one: This one has a wife, I said, this one a new house, that one a job in Germany. But I could not describe who they are—only what they have— and I realized with a start that I do not know them at all, although we lived under the same roof for almost eighteen years. I understood in that instant that you can do things with someone but not share yourself with them, you can be in the same room with someone and not really be *with* them if you do not have a good sense of who you are. And because most of us need time to find out who we are, at least some of our years spent at home are very lonely, regardless of the number of siblings we have around us.

If a child has a stuttering sense of herself or himself—and what adolescent doesn't—home can become a prison and the parents the prison guards, and the child can feel very lonely even among people who care. Most American children who grew up in nuclear families have few adults they can turn to anymore. Uncles, aunts, grandparents often don't live nearby. As a result, the parents' lifestyle, beliefs, and quirks have a tremendous impact on the children's lives. If children feel upset or troubled by their parents, even the privacy of a bedroom is no escape. Furthermore, if children spend too much time alone, the parents begin to worry about their health. Children need family contact and intimacy, but parents tend to forget their children also need to be alone. They need to touch themselves, look at themselves in mirrors, and develop a sense of themselves that will make them feel whole, autonomous, and special. When children say "Leave me alone!" they mean it.

Sometimes, when we are children, we believe if we feel lonely and misunderstood at home we will feel better once we move somewhere else. We believe, mistakenly, that by leaving our farms and small towns and suburbs and moving to the city we will be transformed from a bored person to an exciting one, or we hope that by leaving the city for the suburbs or small towns we will be transformed from a nervous creature to a serene one, from fragmented into whole.

Childhood

I couldn't wait to get out of the farm town where I was reared. Although I lived there for eighteen years, I did not grow there. I grew up later, by myself. I was very surprised when the isolation I felt in that town followed me to Chicago and New York, surprised to find out that we carry our boredom and our loneliness with us wherever we go. Mordecai Richler wrote about this when he said of his native Canada: ". . . the truth is if we were indeed hemmed in by the boring, the inane and the absurd, we foolishly blamed it all on Canada, failing to grasp that we would suffer from a surfeit of the boring, the inane and the absurd wherever we eventually settled and would carry Canada with us everywhere and for good measure." We carry our loneliness and anxiety from Topeka to Fire Island to Sausalito. It shadows us, much as we try to shake it.

We tend to blame our parents for our woes, even though we know the chains of our loneliness and discontent are tied not to our parents but walls within ourselves and that breaking into this prison is more dangerous than breaking out. Some of us break free internally and never out loud. Some of us must confront our parents. In either case, it is a difficult time for all involved.

A friend of mine sat by my fireplace one day and told me about her last visit home, when she had finally told her mother how she felt. After a few days at home, she had locked herself in her bedroom and her mother stood outside the door yelling at her. Finally, my friend unlocked the door, came out, and said: "Let's talk."

Her mother said: "You don't love me. You never loved me. You kissed your father when you came off the plane but you didn't kiss me. You've always been that way."

My friend said to me: "My mother believes she gave her life for her children. When they invented permanent press she was out of a job." Her face was pale and strained in the fire's glow. "She never knew me. I grew up thinking I was unlovable. Now I know she couldn't give me the love I needed. Now I have taken responsibility for myself, and I tell myself she's a woman who happens to be my mother and if it weren't for that we would have nothing in common. I told her: 'Mother, I'm sorry if I hurt you. Maybe we don't love each other, but at least we could respect each other. Maybe that's all we can expect from each other, to treat each other with respect.' I've made my peace with her. Now all I have to do is live with the mother inside of me." She stared at the flames a long time and then she said, "I wish I could crawl under the covers and be a baby and start all over again."

We are sometimes angry as children and angry as adults, and it is unfortunate that most of us don't know what to do with it and so we turn it against ourselves. Those who can get angry know how to love better than those who are always polite, for they know the difference between anger and hate and that is a key to good loving.

Unfortunately, the goal of many parents is to "keep peace in the family." Children obey for no other reason than the way the family is constructed. It is a monarchy, with parents as titular king and queen and the children as serfs—privileged serfs, to be sure, but they depend on their rulers' beneficence for survival. This arrangement doesn't make the family an ideal setting for free expression of emotions. The family is the first major social institution with which a child comes in contact, and the family message often is that it is not wise to say what one thinks, for one might be punished, or worse, ostracized.

One male friend of mine grew up in a family where the rule was: If it hurts, shut up. If it feels good, shut up. You can feel what you want, but just don't express it. His first girlfriend was very emotional. He loved her for it and his parents hated her. After six years of pressure from his family, he finally stopped seeing her and eventually married someone like his mother. I know another man who told me his parents cooperated in their marriage like two factory workers running a machine. This man talks very softly and elegantly, almost in verse, and when he is done I never know quite what he means. His sexual fantasies show a tremendous desire to let go. He wants to find a woman with whom he can lie naked in the moonlight on his queen-sized mattress, kissing and nibbling each other head to toe. The son of rigid parents wants to let loose, and finds he cannot.

I have been in rooms with families whose favorite television programs were comedies in which a husband, wife, and children fight and scream at one another. It astounds me how the viewers of these comedies can laugh about the honest prejudice and open anger on TV, but they cannot turn off the set and take the plunge in their own home. I know a son in Michigan who couldn't blow up at his father and became so repressed that the war in Vietnam became an outlet for him. I have seen a teenage boy at a therapist's office beat to death a pillow that represented his father.

It is difficult to rear a child, but it is more difficult to become an adult. If the parents can give love freely and receive the love that's given, a baby will perceive this and respond. There are some alcoholic women who know how to love, and some respectable schoolteachers who cannot. A social worker may not know the difference, but a child does.

Some psychiatrists use the term "good enough" mother to describe women who are able to love. The good enough mother knows how to hold without grasping, how to comfort without clinging, how to let go without pushing away. When the child tries to squirm off her lap to explore the next room, she allows it, and when the child returns for affection, she willingly takes it once again into her arms. This breaking away and returning, again and again, is crisis and growth, is vulnerability laid open, and so it becomes strength.

Children reared like this are able to be alone in their mother's presence, and whole in the mother's absence, and they become the happiest adults. They have what Guntrip called "sophisticated aloneness." This means they can be solitary without feeling withdrawn, separate without feeling bereft of love.

If parents can give children a sense of themselves, then the children will learn to use loneliness well and will know not to fear it. They can be alone without feeling lonely.

The best parents fill their children's needs: They give them enough attention, teach them how to play, give them affection, respect, and discipline. They do this instinctively, remembering how they would like to be treated if they were children again. Good parents respect their children's wishes to be alone, encourage them to speak freely about what bothers them without judging or mocking. They treat them as young human beings who have all the emotions of adults and just as much despair. These parents teach their children the value of loneliness, separation, and growth.

I met a woman who had such parents. She is fifty-nine years old and has a husband and children who love her and a job that fulfills her. "My mother knew from the day I was born that I was unique," she said. Her voice slowed and softened when she talked about those memories. "If you can give that to your children, you have given them something worth more than diamonds." She was looking at me, but past me, way beyond me, and the child was in her eyes.

How I envy this woman! I was uneasy with the people around me. Adults were mysterious and terrifying creatures, and life seemed overwhelming. Later when my mother and I talked about my childhood, I remembered those times of loneliness, terror, mistakes, embarrassments, and regret, but she remembered the good times, the laughter and fun. Somewhere, between our two versions of those early years, lies the truth about one child's world. A world that prepared me for loneliness.

4

Romantics and Masochists

"Every woman adores a Fascist,
The boot in the face, the brute
Brute heart of a brute like you."
(Poet and Author Sylvia Plath, "Daddy")

Each time we dance close to someone we care for, each time we cry over a love scene in the theater, each time we gaze into a lover's eyes, we are acting out a romanticism we learned about when we were very young. Romantics are lonely because they cannot relate realistically to people. They believe in a world of grand gestures. They live in a fairy-tale world. People are images and symbols to them, and each time the real world intervenes, their dreams crumble.

In nineteenth and early twentieth century classics, the tragic lover is often portrayed as feeling a "splendid loneliness," but this is not what I am talking about. The loneliness of the modern romantic is pitiful rather than splendid, and the pain is very real. Often, romantics are even afraid of real love and develop a pattern of failed relationships to protect their fears. By keeping people at arm's length, they become self-destructive and even masochistic. While complaining that they are lonely, they continue to do the very things that make them lonely in the first place.

A driving restlessness begins when we are around eight years old. We begin to look for a close friend, someone to love. By this time, no matter how anxious we are about being rejected and abandoned, we are even more anxious about being alone without friends. Our need for others is so strong that we overcome our fears and find a "best friend." Often, our first friend symbolizes or idealizes something we admire. She or he may be the fastest runner in the class or be driven to school in a yellow sports car. We like them not so much for who they are but for what they represent. This is often how a romantic is born. Friends, and later, lovers, are ideals rather than real people. We all pass through this stage, but the romantic hangs onto it and doesn't progress to more real relationships.

In adolescence, this pattern continues. If we can find no one to attach ourselves to, we succumb to what Robert Weiss calls "objectless pining." We brood and fantasize, sleep a lot, lose or gain weight, and our parents shake their heads and say they don't know what is wrong.

Octavio Paz explains it this way: "It is true that we sense our aloneness almost as soon as we are born. But children and adults can transcend their solitude and forget themselves in games or work. The adolescent, however, vacillates between infancy and youth, halting for a moment before the infinite richness of the world. He is astonished at the fact of his being and this astonishment leads to reflection: as he leans over the river of his consciousness, he asks himself if the face that appears there, disfigured by the water, is his own. The singularity of his being . . . becomes a problem and a question . . ." This fantasizing leads the adolescent into a dream world.

Romantics and Masochists

Adolescence is such a vulnerable time, we so desperately need someone to identify with, that we seek out heroes to help us along. This is when girls develop crushes on their teachers and boys follow the star athletes around.

The betrayals and slights we would ignore as adults take on ominous proportions, so great is the adolescents' need to live in a world that never disappoints them. A thirty-three-year-old businessman was asked by a therapist when he last cried. The man replied without hesitation: "When I didn't make the freshman basketball team in high school."

The singer Janis Joplin, because she was unpopular, was not invited to her high school prom. She spoke of this "tragedy" even after her success, and became, on stage, queen of a hundred proms before she died. Hitler's adolescent dream, say his biographers, was to be a city planner and build towns—a dream that was crushed when his plans for a new opera house in Linz were ignored. Instead of rebuilding towns, he tried, in his brutal way, to rebuild a society. But even his distorted victories could not soothe that early defeat. While waiting in a bunker during the final days before his death, he put the last touches on those plans for his opera house. When adolescent dreams are thwarted, as with Joplin and her high school proms, the man who didn't make the basketball team, and Hitler's architectural plans, it hurtles us into loneliness as surely as if we had tripped headlong over an unseen root.

Considering the vulnerability of the adolescent, it is a wonder we survive to adulthood. It is an unforgiving time. We never forgive ourselves or those we idealize for not living up to the dream. It seems to me, in retrospect, that I was running a constant fever then. Not the physical kind, but the emotional kind, such that everything and everyone was intensified. I was alternately ecstatic and in despair. Each infatuation seemed like true love. Sex, love, and romanticism all became interchangeable.

On Loneliness

The memory of our first love never goes away. A sixty-three-year-old woman described her first date to me the other day as if it happened yesterday. "He called me at home. I can't imagine anything these days that would create the kind of bliss that telephone call did. We went to a dance and on the way home, in the back seat of the car, he held my hand. As simple as that was, it was sheer ecstasy. I felt, and I was right, that life would never hold anything more than that. I have had all sorts of pleasures since, but nothing compares to that first time. That feeling is never possible again."

If we had a good experience when we were sixteen, we try to recreate it when we are thirty-six or sixty. If we had a bad experience, we keep searching for what we thought we missed. Even if we grow out of romanticism, there are tremendous social pressures to conform to its ideals and treat them as fact rather than fantasy. We expect some romanticism in our lives—the songs and films of our youth told us it would be so. When our lives don't turn out the way we had been promised they would, the effects on us can be devastating.

An older friend told me that every time he thought of high school, he thought of a song by by 1950's teen idol Bobby Vinton. "Blue, blue, blue—the connotation that it is not a good thing to be alone and lonely, that we must stay away from it, and so we have Valentine's Day and fortieth wedding anniversaries and romanticized wars and wasn't-it-great-in-high-school and God-what-a-prom, and meanwhile the night of senior prom I personally went home and tried to kill myself."

He paused and lit a cigarette; his hand was trembling. "I tell you, missing someone was beautiful, feeling the need for someone else was beautiful, but it was all unrealistic. We felt comfortable with the illusion until it became clear it *was* an illusion, and then we were left with this tremendous empty void and we were frightened and still didn't know what happened."

These emotions sometimes panic us when we are young. They fill us like air fills a balloon, stretching us taut until we become afraid we will burst. But we do not explode. We usually implode instead, into a tight solid core, like black holes in space—little human stars collapsing into ourselves under enormous pressure, becoming a mass so dense that not even our little light can shine.

We look for something, someone to believe in so we can believe more easily in ourselves. In the rural Midwest where I grew up, some of us tried to find ourselves again with new loves in the back seats of cars on rutted moonlit roads. Others tried to find themselves again in the war-adrenaline of football fields or with beer and drugs behind the barn. I left home with that old Beatles' song, "She's Leaving Home," in my heart. The song describes a girl sneaking out of her bedroom at 5 a.m. having left a note that she "hoped would say more" on the kitchen table, stepping into freedom. Most parents fail to understand that ritualized rebellion is as predictable as a cheap romance novel and that for some people, running away is the only way they can find themselves.

Much of the reason why we feel lonely in love is rooted in what we experienced in childhood and adolescence. From the very beginning, boys and girls are taught to react differently toward love.

Psychologists have observed that when young boys begin to live out fantasies about their mothers or help in the kitchen and cling to them, they are quickly ridiculed, called a "momma's boy" and sent outside. They are discouraged from being too attached to their mother. They learn to suppress their feelings. Rivalries with fathers become "friendly," neutralized, rechanneled through other competitive areas such as sports. Frustrations are diluted, or at least more easily ignored, as their worlds broaden.[*]

---

[*] See footnote, page one, gender identity and orientation.

Boys soon learn to remain detached, hide real feelings, and even become more tentative in relationships with women. One result is that they can feel lonely in love—unable to open up or to give—and often don't even realize they are cutting off their emotions. It is a pattern that may continue throughout life.

When girls begin to live out their fantasies, however, they are encouraged. When a girl takes her father's hand, sits on his lap, flirts with him, she is not ridiculed. On the contrary, she is rewarded with smiles and called "daddy's little girl." While a boy's fantasies are dispersed, a girl's fantasies are allowed to stay focused. A sense of rivalry with her mother continues and often increases. A daddy's girl eventually turns into a woman-child who is grateful for a man's kindness.

I have heard so many women, myself included, describe the major attribute of a new lover as being the fact that he is "so good" to her. She is grateful to find a man who is as benevolent to her as her father once was, who will treat her as the child she still longs to be, who will take care of her—an emotion that can be buried in even the deepest feminist.

Because girls and boys develop emotionally at a different rate, many girls remain longer in unrealistic romantic situations. They tend to fantasize about boys their age, who are usually incapable of responding to their emotional needs. Girls go through puberty earlier than boys, and, as psychiatrist Harry Stack Sullivan says, this leads to a "peculiar sort of stutter in development."

The traditional heterosexual love dance begins for girls as a frustrating cycle of desire and neglect with boys their age. A high school boy once complained to me: "If I date a girl a few times, she thinks I must love her. Girls think life is a soap opera. I'm just out for a good time."

To resolve this dilemma, girls use sex to get love and boys pretend love to get sex, and we are off and running. To this day I may feel calm, integrated, content, productive, and then fall apart when my lover does not call. It has nothing to do with reality; it has to do with my fantasies when I was twelve years old. A silent phone is a rejection; the more I feel rejected the more I am sure it must be love. After all, if it hurts so much, it must be because I care so much.

It is tempting to blame the infant years of movies and stars—think Humphrey Bogart, Doris Day—for this romanticism that makes us lonely even in love. Hollywood's early role-modeling of what constitutes "love" seduced our parents and grandparents into false versions of reality—and those fantasies, passed from generation to generation, linger on. From an early age, I diligently clipped poems about women with bruised hearts, usually written by men, which are now hoarded in boxes in the attic. I used to read the short stories about romantic angst in *Redbook* and listen to old Johnny Mathis records at night alone in my room, gazing out the window for effect. In my dreams, I remembered the swirl of Scarlett O'Hara's white dress and Rhett Butler's gaze at the bottom of the stairs.

I didn't know that I was already staring into the distorted looking glass through which men and women from early on view each other and set up a lifetime reflection of mutual loneliness and disappointment. I didn't know that romantics tend to act out their old fantasies on whomever they love. Each new love makes them surge and suffer equally because each new love triggers the same old responses.

Romantics sometimes tend to be attracted to people with similar looks—to men with black hair and square chins, or tall thin blondes. They are drawn to lovers not because of who the lover is, but because of what illusions that person represents. It is as if two people do an emotional dance with each other: They don't touch, don't do the same step; they turn and dance with other people, each moving separately until the dance is over; then they turn and go their separate ways, not having made contact at all.

Romantics also tend to categorize people as lovers, potential lovers, and nonlovers. They behave differently when they are with people who they want to have sex with than they do with people who are "just friends." In doing this, romantics cut a lot of people from their lives. They shortchange friends by altering plans whenever a lover calls; they make it clear that other people are second. They shortchange potential lovers—and themselves—by trying to project a false image of themselves, instead of just being who they really are. They exclude former lovers from their lives, for former lovers are a living memorial that the romantic misjudges and misperceives.

Romantics are unforgiving if you step out of the dream. Romantic endings are often merciless on both sides, a sort of bludgeoning back to reality. The poet James Reed writes:

> . . . and here's the horror—
> You have to dismantle the heavenly apparatus,
> the whole absurd structure
> you inflated so quickly out of thinnest air
> (and bad judgment)
> into a palatial backload of bricks—
> and down they do come,
> like New York collapsing,
> brick by brick.
> It's sad—
> that you nearly always
> have to throw a few
> at whoever it was
> you turned into God.

Romanticism and masochism often go hand in hand, because romantics enjoy being martyrs to the cause of love. Romantics need to hurt. They feel comfortable being victims. When we are lonely in life, we can always blame our parents, who didn't ask us if we wanted to be born. But when we are lonely in love, we often have no one to blame but ourselves. Because we romantics don't want to face this unpleasant reality, we hold our lovers responsible for our loneliness. We wire our relationships to self-destruct. We lie and deceive. Romanticism is based on lies: lies that our fathers told us, lies our mothers told us, and lies we like to tell ourselves when we find it convenient.

Perhaps one reason sadomasochists make us uncomfortable is because they flirt with pain on a physical level, which is similar to what some of us do on an emotional level. In sadomasochism (SM) sex, the other person becomes an object (this is why masks are often a part of SM). It's the ritual of sex that counts, not the person you do the ritual with. In SM sex, pain brings pleasure, just as it does for romantic masochists on an emotional level. In both cases, people have a vested interest in the pain.

It is not too difficult to figure out why women are romantic masochists: First, there is their experience in childhood and adolescence; next, there is a pattern of distrust across several generations of women, an inherited message that men—with their, power, freedom, and hormones—will hurt you.

Mothers of past generations often wanted to be remembered best for how they suffered and sacrificed themselves for their families and their men. Many daughters followed their mothers' example: It is the only way they know how to relate to men. Mothers of children growing up in the 1950s and 1960s were perhaps the most frustrated generation of women that American culture has ever produced. Many of these mothers were the first American women to perceive the possibilities of doing something with their lives besides cleaning house and breeding children. But few of them had the education, the moral support, or the opportunity to do so. Some of these women took jobs, but the jobs were often not equal to their capabilities. They got a taste of new freedom but little chance to explore it. They resented their husbands' freedom and took out their frustrations on their daughters. Many of their daughters got the warning: Men will disappoint you—which was was just another way of saying that life will disappoint you.

But romanticism and its sometime companion—masochism—are not for women only. Far from it! Men, after all, were reared by the same parents and also learned how to hurt and be hurt by love. The male romantic idealizes the person he thinks he loves, just as the female romantic does. Like her, he balks at becoming involved in—or staying in—a down-to-earth relationship, and he is willing to sacrifice himself over and over to the romantic dream.

The male romantic has an additional burden: He often feels he must be the aggressor in a romantic situation. Most women feel they should be passive and submissive, which causes its own brand of suffering. But for the man, constant pursuit and occasional rejection are no less agonizing than waiting for an unanswered text message.

Unfortunately, I fall to pieces over romantic men who are masochists. Every man I have loved, with one exception, has believed in the myths of pain and loss. We always make a fine team. How we pine! We dredge the depths. How we feed each other's guilt!

I remember sitting in a restaurant listening to a lover explain why he was leaving me for another woman. "I feel comfortable, feel at home, with her," he said. Then he took my hand across the table and looked into my eyes. "But I love you in a different way. With you I feel lyrical; you are poetry to me." There was silence. I felt like Tragedy; he was breaking my heart. "It may be," I said, "that you are my first poem." At the time, it seemed appropriate. I used to call this romanticism, but there was more than a tinge of masochism there. The suffering was real, it was painful, and it hurt all the way.

I saw a 1940s movie on TV called *Now, Voyager,* which was typical of the kind of romantic, masochistic sentiment women of that generation embraced when they were young. In the movie, Bette Davis stars as the unwanted child of a wealthy family. She has a nervous breakdown and is sent to a sanitarium. After her recovery, she goes on a world cruise during which she falls in love with Paul Henreid's character, a married man. It is implied that his wife is an ogre. They fall in love, but divorce was not an option for a respectable family man. The two agree to part.

Bette returns to her family, dates a number of eligible, rich bachelors, but does not marry them: She cannot forget the man she met on the cruise. Every day she wears his favorite flower, the camellia.

Years later she meets Paul unexpectedly at a party and learns that his twelve-year-old daughter is in the same sanitorium where she was once treated. He tells her that his wife has rejected the daughter and does not want her back. Bette goes to the sanitorium, gracefully wheedles her way into the child's heart, and when the treatment is done, takes the girl home with her. Paul arrives at Bette's front door and takes back his child because, he says, he does not want Bette to sacrifice her life for him.

In the final scene, they face each other in her library, unable to touch or display their love openly. Instead, Paul lights two cigarettes and passes one to her. Bette takes a puff. She says the girl will be "their" child and he can come and visit them any time. But, Paul asks her, can they ever hope for true happiness between them? "Well," Bette says, exhaling a long drag of cigarette smoke, "don't let's ask for the moon. We've got the stars."

For decades this was the typical movie industry recipe for romance. By the end of the film, everybody is trapped by everyone else's self-sacrifice. No one grows, no one is loved realistically. Not only Hollywood is responsible for this distortion of love. Think back to the classic love stories—Sir Launcelot and Guinevere, Romeo and Juliet, Heathcliff and Cathy. Most of them involve masochism. These were the tenets of true love set up for us. This was the seductive martyrdom we learned from our culture and parents, and only by breaking the mold do we not bequeath it to our children.

When I thought of this movie, I remembered a friend of mine and her eight-year-old daughter. They were hooking a rug together one Sunday when I visited.

"What do children want?" my friend asked her daughter.

"Children want the sky," the daughter answered, not looking up from her work.

"What do men want?" the mother asked.

"Men want penises," the girl answered.

"Well," said the mother, a little taken aback, "what do women want?"

"Women want hell," the child answered without dropping a stitch. I couldn't help but hope that this child, because she recognizes the symptoms when she is eight, will be able to outgrow it by the time she has children of her own.

"Love," said James Baldwin in a conversation with friends, "is being at the mercy of someone else." This is a good description of romantic love—of giving up your freedom, of turning your life over to someone else for safekeeping. We are all to some extent emotionally needy and dependent.

But "it is one thing to recognize one's dependence and limitations, and it is something entirely different to indulge in this dependence, to worship the forces on which one depends," said social philosopher and psychoanalyst Erich Fromm. "To understand realistically and soberly how limited our power is is an essential part of wisdom and of maturity; to worship it is masochistic and self-destructive. The one is humility, the other self-humiliation."

Many women I know, myself included, do not know how to go about recognizing our dependency so we won't be crucified by it. We are both afraid of loneliness, of being swallowed up in our inner emptiness, and afraid of a close relationship that would overwhelm us and rob us of our personality. Guntrip described this same phenomenon in a schizophrenic patient. She has "no well-assured sense of her own selfhood, so is unable to make satisfactory relationships with other people . . . She doesn't feel strong enough to withstand any close relationship and maintain a viable personality . . . but neither can she do without the human relationship she needs."

This low self-image has little relation to what people "do" in life, what jobs we hold, how much property we own, how much prestige we feel we have. In private conversations, I have heard some of the most intelligent, talented, and attractive people in the country say that their lives would be fine if only they were able to love realistically.

The aim of the masochist, says Eric Fromm, is to lose one's self to a bigger and more powerful cause, to fuse, to give one's self over to someone else in the belief that through them they will be strengthened. As Fromm puts it, the masochist feels: "As long as I struggle between my desire to be independent and strong, and my feeling of insignificance or powerlessness, I am caught in a tormenting conflict. If I can succeed in reducing my individual self to nothing, if I can overcome the awareness of my separateness as an individual, I may save myself from this conflict."

Still, we cling to the dreams that destroy us. A young schoolteacher I know was convinced the right man could make her life complete. She found him and married him. Being a romantic, she chose her image of an ideal man. Not being a realist, she did not look behind that facade to see who he really was. He was a handsome and brilliant person who was totally self-centered. He remembered everything he ever read but did not bother to think about her needs. Her love became a trap, her prince became her jailor. But she refused to face the fact that her romantic dream was bankrupt. She ignored the panic of her emptiness and hurt by deadening all feeling. She became emotionally and physically numb. It was not until she burned herself under a scalding shower that she faced how serious her situation was. Then she saw what she had done, saw that she had given him total power over her. Her fear of feeling lonely made her want to cling to him and at the same time her fear of seeming too dependent on him had gradually made her withdraw.

As Ernest Becker writes in *The Denial of Death:* "We enter symbiotic relationships in order to get the security we need, in order to get relief from our anxieties, our alone-ness and help-lessness; but these relationships also bind us, they enslave us even further because they support the lie we have fashioned. So we strain against them in order to be more free."

We all go through a sort of mourning when our illusions die. Some of us react in an extreme way, as my schoolteacher friend did, and some recognize it sooner and seek help. The strength of our reactions depends on how deeply we are submerged in our romantic myths.

People who settle for romanticism also settle for infatuation, excitement, and dependency, and none of this is love. Some would argue it is not as good as love. But romantics believe it is better than love, for where love may plateau for a day or week, romanticism scales to great heights and crashes into ravines and makes us feel alive—which is why most romantics would not give up their pain and fantasies for anything in the world.

In his book on suicide, A. Alvarez writes that when the London police haul corpses out of the Thames, they can always tell who committed suicide for love and who has killed himself for debts, because the "fingers of the lovers are almost invariably lacerated by their attempts to save themselves by clinging to the piers of the bridges. In contrast, the debtors apparently go down like slabs of concrete."

What we do to ourselves with romanticism is sometimes terrible. We use it in the name of love with the same cool logic that we bomb for peace. In fact, romanticism has nothing to do with love or even romance. Romance is a prelude to love; romanticism replaces love. It turns love into a skirmish and people into willing victims. The outcome of the skirmish is predetermined. The romantics will win by losing, and in losing, get what they need: fireworks and fugues, more intrigue than Hitchcock, more brilliance than the sun, more tragedy than *War and Peace*. Romantics like the chase, and when you begin to respond, they often back away because they are afraid of love, which is not nearly as exciting and a lot more work.

We can unlearn destructive romantic habits, but only if we are willing to face our essential loneliness and to disappoint, even hurt, other people to free ourselves. We cannot escape the pattern of romanticism by meditating alone in a room, despite the known benefits of meditation. Escape comes only from interaction with other people, from experimenting in relationships. It comes from doing what we've never been able to do before and then seeing what happens and how we feel. It comes in learning to say no when before we would have said yes, in learning to speak up when once we were silent, in learning to accept people when once we tried to change them, or hoped they would change themselves to be what we wanted them to be. It comes from making mistakes—a lot of mistakes—sometimes ones that make us seem unnecessarily cruel, irrational, even whimsical in our actions and our ways of loving.

Unfortunately, we are afraid of what would happen if we admitted our way of loving was wrong, afraid of tearing down to the bone all the illusions we believed in and lived by, afraid of the raw hurt. Nothing blocks change like fear.

It helps to recognize that most of us have needs that can never be filled, needs that come out of old childhood fears. We must, for a start, be content with what lovers can give us rather than be miserable about all they can never give. We must try, in our relationships, to identify our emotions point by point: Now I am feeling this way—why? Now that way—why? And we must keep doing this until we stop living by our old and useless patterns. We must be very sure of what we want and what we need. We must remember that we always desire most that which we cannot have, and that the ones who got away may not have been our greatest loves, after all. I believe true love can free us, but I know romanticism can only trap us. When we let romanticism become a burden, when we let those we love become our masters, then we are masochists. We always resent those who control us, especially when the key they hold is the one to our hearts.

To be able to break the pattern handed down from parent to child—to be able to say: "stop it"—enables us to love. To know that adoration is not love and passion is not love and dependency is not love and even orgasm is not love enables us to clear the pathways that might lead to real love. If people can feel whole by themselves, then the neurotic needs they bring to a relationship may evaporate, and people will be together because they want to be and not because they expect something from each other.

5

Sex

"I have been faithful to thee, Cynara! in my fashion."
Non sum qualis eram bonae sub regno Cynarae
(Author and Poet Ernest Dowson's poem about hopeless longing)

After I left my husband, I slept with men more for the affection than the sex, though the sex was often good just the same. I enjoyed the orgasms but needed the touching and holding. I didn't sleep with strangers or men I didn't like. I didn't go in for anonymous sex. But neither did I sleep only with men I loved.

I got along all right this way until I asked a man to sleep with me, and he said no. He was looking for something else, he said.

The man and I are friends now. Over dinner one night a few months later he explained that by saying no to me he was saying yes to himself and his other needs. He was reared in a family where the men didn't cry, didn't laugh, and didn't love. Now, with the help of therapy, he was beginning to feel real emotion, and one of the things he felt was that for him sex was aggression, a form of attack against women. This is not uncommon. There is certainly truth in the phrase "war between the sexes" and we all know that "make love, not war" means "make sex, not war"—for sex often channels passions that are paralleled in war.

On Loneliness

Until he could start using sex in a more positive way, he did not want to sleep with me. All of this made him a lonely man.

"I can alleviate my physical aloneness easily," he said. "I sleep with women I am not close to and in that moment of orgasm when I blot out my mind and cut into the center of my being I feel good, but then the vacuum comes back again and I am lonely."

I watched this kind and struggling man earnestly leaning forward across the table from where I sat and felt sorry for us both. I have slept with too many men who have meant too much and he has slept with too many women who have meant too little, and it ends up the same. The circle closes: We ache for physical love but are unable to pay the emotional price. We are lonely if we do and lonely if we don't. Now what? If we, in some moment of future weakness, had sex anyway, it would be a perpetuation of both my masochism and his. I understood—and it saddened me to understand—that we were closer facing each other across that tabletop than we would ever be facing each other across rumpled sheets. I have curled up on warm rocks and sunbathed nude with a male friend and neither of us felt embarrassed or possessive. But if sexual acts are ever committed, suddenly territorial rights are at stake and something is owed.

The pros and cons of sex without love have been debated without end—both in cities, where it can be hard to meet people, and in the countryside, where everyone knows everyone else. As a result, the question is so muddied that it is hard to see at all. In the cheering corner are some enlightened liberals, feminists, swingers, and chauvinists. In the booing corner are parents of daughters, romantics, every established religion, and idealists. Sex, it seems, makes strange bedfellows.

Those who study these problems say sex without love cannot alleviate long-term loneliness. They say we must first learn how to connect with people—learn to overcome inhibitions and defenses—before the sex will improve.

But sex without love has, all in all, been good for me. It has helped me separate the two and taught me that sex without love does not necessarily mean sex without communication, affection, and caring. Sex without love—but with the right time, place, person, and expectations—is one way to untangle us from the myths that chain sex and love together. It teaches us the difference between sex and love. Each is good separately, but better together, once we have learned they are not one and the same.

Most of us need sex just as babies need to be held by mothers. When we don't get sex, we can get caught up in loneliness that only one thing can cure, just as only food can cure a hunger pain.

Most of us conveniently forget that our sensuousness emerged even before we were able to walk and that a lot of our early play was sex play. These sexual urges are forbidden or diverted in our early years. We may not forget our first feeling of lust, but we usually keep it locked away. As we grow older, if we continue to ignore, repress, or deny our sexuality, we can create tension in the body to the point where we cannot concentrate at work or truly love, a tension that masturbation can alleviate but not help in the long run. The rare exception might be Buddhist and Hindu monks and and other spiritual gurus who, through decades of practice, sublimate the sex drive. The rest of us, however, can become obsessed with its lack. I remember a few years of deprivation in New York when I would find myself forlornly sneaking glances at the crotches of men opposite me on subways, wondering about their penises.

A few years earlier, because I was interested in how alienation across a range of psychological levels can lead to rage, especially in men, I wrote a story for a magazine that included interviewing men held in a unit for sex offenders in East Jersey State Prison.

Most of these men had little or no sex education as children. Some were raped or molested as children, and some said that, even in a loving relationship or marriage, they had never had sex without feelings of confusion and guilt. Oscar M., who had raped thirteen women, told me: "The rapes weren't sexual. I could have had better orgasms if I had gone into the bathroom and taken care of myself. I just hated myself and wanted someone else to hate me."

While leaving the scene of his last rape, he was chased by a cop who pointed a Magnum pistol at his chest. Oscar knew at that moment how badly he wanted to die. He reached for his knife, hoping the cop would shoot him. "I wanted him to squeeze that bullet out," he said. "But he looked at me a few seconds and then he holstered his gun. He knew I wanted to die and wouldn't give it to me."

After talking to these rapists, I went home and crawled under the covers and shivered because the men I had spoken to that day were articulate, soft-spoken, good-looking, and in a different time and place I could perhaps have become involved with someone just like them. They reminded me of my mistakes, for sex without self-esteem can be a form of self-abnegation, self-destruction, and I have slept with men who did not value me because I did not value myself.

When we are lonely, it is sometimes difficult to remember that sex itself is neutral, and that you alone decide whether you will use it in a positive or negative way. Children instinctively turn it into fun; it feels good and that is why they play sexual games. All primates rehearse sex play as infants. John Money, medical psychologist at Johns Hopkins University, said that if you deprive monkeys of sex play during the first year of life, they never learn how to copulate. It is unfortunate that most societies and religions punish childhood sexuality and encourage rigid sexual taboos, which Dr. Money calls "the graven image of the groin." Like it or not, it is part of our heritage along with apple pie.

In some other cultures, adults feel sex play among children is a necessary part of growing up. In our culture, even when playing with blocks on the nursery floor, children act out their sexuality. Boys have a tendency to erect towers and other tall structures, while girls tend to build enclosures, rooms, and houses. It is hard to tell whether social training or biological instinct causes this difference, but it is also hard to deny that boys are phallic builders and girls prefer inner spaces that are entered and exited or filled and emptied. Is this vaginal politics? I wonder what would happen if you forbade girls to build rooms and forced them to build towers? Would they be more aggressive females, or would it backfire, causing them to lose a sound sexual sense of themselves? Would they like their bodies better or like boys less? Would they prefer to be on top during sex? Or none of these?

We don't know. All we know for sure is that as children we get what we can where we can, and we usually find out about our sexuality when we sleep at a friend's house or go to summer camp. At my Wisconsin Girl Scout camp, counselors arranged a "dance party" on the final night, and had us draw straws to see if we would go as a boy or a girl. (There was a boys' camp nearby but we were not allowed to mix.) The girls who dressed as boys were expected to invite a real girl as their date. To my relief, I drew a girl straw. Afterward, I sat by the river and "necked" with my date, who excelled at playing a cute boy.

But no matter how we find out about our bodies, it almost always makes us anxious. As a child, a priest told me to confess every time I kissed a boy "longer than I would kiss my father."

Dr. Money calls this "sex above the belt" and "sex below the belt": "Sex above the belt is lyrical, love, romantic, wonderful, and you're allowed to do it as a teenager. Sex below the belt is filthy, sinful, carnal, nasty, dirty, and don't-touch-it-but-save-it-for-the-one-you-love." He says that "the major assignment for every adolescent growing up in our society is to reconcile the two. No wonder sex creates problems."

In the past, when marriages were arranged, there was much less confusion between sex and love. People married for convenience, survival, title, money, or land, and could satisfy their sexual needs elsewhere, especially men. They didn't confuse the commitments of marriage with sex or love.

But America, with its many Protestant middle-class traditions, has always been an above-the-belt, below-the-belt land. We refuse to sever sex from love as if the separation would kill them both. Philip Slater in his book *The Pursuit of Loneliness* and others have argued that by linking love with sex we have created an important natural resource: frustration. We have produced an artificial sexual scarcity by believing we must be in love to have sex. We rechannel our sexual energies to release our sexual tensions. We produce, consume, buy, sell, build, tear down, move, and in general maintain a busy schedule to avoid the thing that bothers us.

By restricting one of the most basic of human needs—sex—we fan the flames of our discontent and work harder and harder for gratification in other areas. We attach sexual interest to nonsexual objects that also elevate our pheromones—like cars, homes, clothing, and promotions. In doing so, we feel empty, lonely, and dissatisfied, even though our lives seem comfortable and full on the surface.

I believe Slater is right, that sex and love are two separate issues and shouldn't be confused with each other, but every time I have good sex with someone I care about, I think I am in love again. I take all the insight and sound advice and roll it up in a little ball and stash it in the back of the closet. Once the affair is over, I play it safe and sleep with men I know I could never love. Then I tire of the safety of it all, and venture toward love again; for love, despite all its self-deceptions, is better than no love at all. I have had good sex with men I care about and men I love. I have had bad sex with men I care about and love. I have had good sex with men I didn't care about. Sex and love are hopelessly entangled in my mind, and sometimes in my confusion, I settle for the loneliness of celibacy.

The problem in all this is learning to focus our needs, as did the man who told me no thanks to the sex but yes, thanks, to the friendship. We must learn what is good for us and what flattens us out. While true of my experiences with men, people of all sexual orientations can make love to a host of people until they are blue in the face and still not be liberated from loneliness.

One weekend I was a guest at a friend's house. Another guest arrived late, so he and I talked only briefly. I woke up in the night to find this man standing by my bed in the dark, smoking a cigarette. I pretended to be asleep. He put out his cigarette in the ashtray and lay down beside me. I pretended to wake up. "Just let me lie here," he said. He moved closer. I was so frightened that I was unable to say anything until he touched me, and then I screamed at him to get out. He laughed, got up from my bed, and sauntered from the room. I barred the door with a chair. The next morning I talked with my friends about it, and he was asked to leave.

Now that I know more about this man, I believe he chose to act this way, in part, due to loneliness and desolation. His wife had left him, he had lost his job, and he was desperately reaching out for someone—anyone. But he didn't understand that you don't make friends by fucking them out of frustration.

On Loneliness

I have met several people like this, people so panicked by loneliness, so intense with their needs, that they drive others away from them. In New York, I had dinner twice with a man who couldn't keep his hands off me. He said we had to sleep together before we could be friends. It was all or nothing and so, for us, it was nothing. Both of these men, and other men and women like them, create their own solitary confinements without any help from the rest of us. They confuse sex with closeness. Many people, because they are desperate with their loneliness, simply are not sensitive about where to draw the line. The loneliness leads them into situations they should not be in simply because they mistakenly believe that being with anyone is better than being alone. However, this kind of sex often ends in emptiness—a sort of emotional hangover that makes you want to fold up inside yourself to prevent those soft inner spaces from any further wear and tear.

For a while, following several love affairs that hurt, I thought of myself as essentially asexual. At this point, I decided to give up on men. It seemed at the time that I had a better rapport with women, and many of them had also been hurt by men. I thought one way to share tenderness would be to have an affair with a woman. This was not a spontaneous idea—at the time, the media had been publicizing bisexuality for months.

I had read a letter in the *Village Voice* on this very subject. The letter said: "Heterosexuality is an illness characterized by impotence, instability, immaturity, promiscuity, and the inability to form loving relationships with either sex." That certainly seemed to ring a bell.

I knew a woman who was willing to try it. I was fascinated by her cascading black hair, the planes of her cheekbones, the hollows of her long neck, the fragile bones of her shoulders. I was, in a way, intimidated by her beauty and mystery. But out of fear, indifference, or perhaps just a lingering uneasiness, I failed to commit myself and nothing ever happened.

Later, I saw how affairs between people of all sexual identities and preferences can be as poisoned by jealousy and fear as heterosexual affairs. Plunging into an affair with a woman—who I thought could fill the emptiness in my life—is exactly what I would do with a man—with the same bitter results. I realized that my individual need would define that relationship, not my identity as a woman or a man.

A female friend once asked me, perplexed, if lesbianism was really the answer. "I can't accept it," she said. After a moment, I answered that neither could I—not until I had completely given up on men. She paused and then said something that changed my entire perspective on sexuality. She said: "Just because you sleep with a woman doesn't mean you give up on all men, any more than sleeping with one man means you have given up on all other men." I waver and wonder.

I cannot help but admire those who have broken through this sexual barrier and experienced the expansive possibilities of everyone's sexuality. I regard them with envy. It is because of my ignorance, distrust of men, and confusion about myself that I end up in lonely corners with my guard up.

For instance, it took me a long time to understand why I was aroused as a teenager by pictures of women in my mother's hidden *Playboy* magazines. Now I know I was responding to the "object" of the woman who was a fantasy, airbrushed to perfection and deliberately seductive. I was fascinated to see women in the nude for the first time, given my culture in which the naked female body—including my own, which had begun to menstruate—was dirty, imperfect, and a source of shame. I wanted to *be* these beautiful women who flaunted their bodies. They had breasts like mine might one day become (they didn't), and I wanted to project myself onto their images and into their skin. I became the woman herself.

Pictures of nude men do not arouse me or women I know. First, it is surprising to see a man in what is traditionally considered a female pose: passive and receptive. He becomes an object of curiosity rather than of sexuality. Furthermore, many women have been conditioned to respond to male aggression, and the male bodies that are undressed, motionless, and vulnerable with all parts showing are simply not that appealing. People have written PhD theses and won research grants analyzing why this is so for many heterosexual women. If we hetero women could respond sexually by ogling pictures of nude men and using those images for fantasy and masturbation, it could help some of us through lonely times.

For a while, I was intrigued by pornography and bisexuality because I thought they might clear up some of my confusion about sex and love. They didn't. But I did learn it is pleasant to know about your body and other people's bodies; to be familiar and comfortable with our bodies in all situations, including nudity and sex; to accept rolls of fat, hairy arms, or scars. I have noticed that the happiest people, the least lonely ones, the ones who always seem comfortable with themselves, the spontaneous, warm ones—those people seem to look good whether dressed or naked. It is as if they have met their bodies, introduced themselves, and got acquainted while most of us remain judgmental strangers to our bodies, especially in the mirror. Now that I look back, I realize that some of my best lovers may have had unglamorous bodies, but they had tremendous sex appeal. And I never heard one of them say that he wished he could change the way he looked.

Sometimes when we are lonely we think we need sex when what we actually need is affection. If we don't know how to ask for

Sex

affection, then sex becomes the price we pay to get it. One way to learn about affection is to hold your friends and be held by them, to learn to touch and be touched. This kind of love incorporates more than sex. It is not asexual so much as beyond sex. It is the love of a friend you can talk to.

I have had men friends whom I slept with once or twice, out of curiosity and as a way, I suppose, to break down any sexual tension or games between us. But to sleep with your friends is to invite heartache and the worry that, afterwards, the friendship may not be the same. This is not to say that lovers can't also be friends, but I have found that when men begin as friends, it is sometimes difficult to shift gears midway down the stretch. I have a special male friend who talked me into bed, and because I refused to sleep with him again he does not call me anymore. Now the friendship seems scarred beyond healing. Sleeping with him was like sleeping with a relative.

Just as there are those we sleep with but do not love, there are those we love but do not sleep with. This is the land of close friendships, sensuality without sexuality, friendly back rubs that stop at the lowest vertebrae and do not continue down. Warmth and cuddling without an obligation to jump into bed— this, I sometimes think with longing, is the true liberation of feeling.

Adults who grew up in families that hug I suspect have an easier time with some of this. It is time, always time, to learn to embrace a brother, and some of us don't do it until we are thirty or forty, and some of us never do. With a network of touchers behind you, it is more difficult to be desolated, devastated by sex and love. One woman I know, when spurned by her lover, met two friends on the sidewalk on her way home. The friends, after hearing what happened, circled her and rocked her there on the sidewalk, and it was what she needed to feel whole again.

On Loneliness

But it is tricky to draw these boundaries between sex and love, for they give way when you poke them. I take the risks between the two again and again, drawn by the potential of sex as an ultimate passion, a state of mind where we no longer have to pinch ourselves to know that we're alive. It is, as Octavio Paz describes, ". . . a hunger for communion, a will to fall and to die as well as to be reborn. We do not ask it for happiness or repose, but simply for an instant of that full life in which opposites vanish, in which life and death, time and eternity, are united."

I first read Paz while living in Mexico with a man whom I did not love, though we cared a great deal for one another. For three months we shared an apartment in the mountains and did not talk about the future but saturated ourselves with the beauty of each day and occasionally had sex at night. It was the first time I was able to separate sex and affection from love and not mistake one for the other. When it was time for me to leave him, the pain of knowing I was free to leave or stay shot through me at the airport like a lance, and I felt for the first time the full weight of my freedom.

I wanted to believe I was in love again, to cling and shelter, but I knew better, and once you know better there is no going back. I found it strange that I should see, really perceive, the power of this freedom in a country like Mexico, among women who certainly were not free. And though I had been told countless times before, I suddenly understood that the freedom was in my head, just as the shackles of childhood were in my head; even an oppressive society could not touch its core, and it surely helped to know I could leave that oppression whenever I wanted.

And so I carried my new-won freedom with me on the plane to Chicago where I lived then. The sense of it comes and goes, of course, but I saw it once, that freedom, and now I know that it is there, hovering, waiting for me to catch up. I slip and fall on my way, backtrack, I go in circles, but these risks and adventures are the very stuff of life, and not to take chances is to limit your options on ecstasy as well as despair.

The freedom has nothing to do with how many men I sleep with. One of the ways we have botched up our sense of sexual liberation is to equate liberation with the number of our lovers rather than with the quality of the loving. But in fact those who are promiscuous are often running away from intimacy, and those who thrive on orgies are often more lonely among a pile of palpitating bodies than others who sit alone on Saturday nights. It is known that this kind of sex is a distancing maneuver, and people who swing and swap as a way of life do so because it is safe. Antiseptic sex, automatic emotional gates. You can have my car keys, house keys, but not my heart, and barely my interest. "Most people who are heavily into group sex are essentially lonely and afraid of closeness and are very often people who depreciate the other gender, so there is hostility in the sex," a sex therapist told me. It is all taking, no sharing, and each person is preserving their fundamental loneliness.

A New York model I know says she has slept with at least five hundred men. "I'm glad I slept with most of them," she says. "You can screw the same guy ten thousand times but you're bound to learn more if you screw ten thousand different guys. It's like trying different brands of beer," she says. She looks at me with big brown eyes, in that moment, as clear and innocent as a child's. I envy her and yet at the same time don't believe that changing men is as easy as changing sheets. "I screw as a pastime," she says. "We run out of talking, out of wine—so let's fuck, you know? I don't think: I'm giving him my body. Romance doesn't enter into it."

Not everyone, and certainly not me, can be as blasé about our sex lives, and most of us wouldn't want to be. Sexual variety means something else to me. It may at its best teach us to appreciate sexuality, ours and others', without abusing it. It can teach us to not cling to people, or, in the French writer Colette's words, "to admire without coveting, possess all without acquiring." Sex with someone you don't love, and therefore sex without fear of abandonment and loss, can free you to more thoroughly enjoy it with those you do love.

There are, indeed, love affairs that can save a marriage. As Merle Shain writes in *Some Men Are More Perfect Than Others,* "There are men who have found the way to tenderness through other women and having found it, took it to their wives." Not everyone, of course, wants to or needs to make the distinction between sex and love. Sometimes on my rainy days, I wish I could believe sex and love were usually compatible and seldom destructive, and I still hold out hope. Here and there I find people who encourage me.

One of them is Dr. Estelle Ramey, a wise and witty woman who has been happily married to her one and only husband for thirty-five years. In her office one day, she told me what she had learned about sex and love: "We have the kind of brain where nothing, absolutely nothing, persists at a high excitement level. It just can't last at that level, ever, in any relationship. In my day, *For Whom the Bell Tolls* was the big book, and when Maria and Robert Jordan made love, the earth moved. And I remember thinking: 'Jesus, it never moved for me. Other things might have happened, but no skyrockets, no sense of interplanetary voyages.' That's why promiscuity sometimes becomes a thing in itself: You can evoke excitement not by changing the hand-holding but the hand-holdee. But eventually, even the most swinging bachelor wakes in the middle of the night and says: 'Why can't I feel anything after sex? What is love really about?' It reminds me of the old conundrum—in every relationship one always loves more, and which one would you prefer to be? The answer is clear: the one who loves more."

She straightened up in her chair and smiled a motherly smile, a sisterly smile, a knowing smile. "Now we women are being told not to settle for anything less than wild joy in our sexual encounters. That leads to disappointment. It leads to the sense that you're being deprived of something, which can then be translated into alienation. It is the loneliness that follows when the man in bed with you has fallen asleep—the pig."

She laughed. "Now we are told he shouldn't do that. I suppose high expectations are better than no expectations. But the best kind of all are realistic expectations. Which is to say that in anything that lasts, you have to be prepared for trade-offs. The tremendous sexual excitement can't last, but the sexual pleasure can. The sexual warmth can even deepen as life brings you common interests, shared memories. If you're really lucky you can effect maybe one good relationship in a lifetime that has all the components of warmth, sexual excitement, commitment, long-term interests. If you're lucky, damn lucky, it will happen to you."

I thought it had happened to me a couple of times. But sometimes the sex is not enough to salvage the love, and sometimes the love isn't the right variety for nurturing the sex. And sometimes I feel like a burglar twirling the combinations of sex and love like a lock on a safe, listening carefully, trying each digit, waiting for the click that will give me access to still more secrets inside of me, the people I sleep with, and the people I love.

6

Love and Marriage

"Two fears alternate, the one of loneliness,
and the other of bondage."

(Cyril Connolly, The Unquiet Grave)

One Autumn night after an evening writing class, I joined several women for tea in a vegetarian restaurant. One of the women, whom I knew casually, was a widow. She was twenty-four years old. "My husband choked to death while he was on a business trip," she said. "He was eating in a hotel dining room and choked on a piece of meat. He fell facedown onto the plate and he died right there." She took a sip of tea.

"The morning after his death I went out for breakfast and I thought: *This is strange. I'm carrying on as if nothing happened, and he's dead.* I tried to mourn him, but his death just didn't make me unhappy, so I gave it up. If he were still alive, he would be making my life miserable. Now I am free of him." She talked as if an aging cat had been hit by a truck, as if the death were a blessing in disguise. But her husband had been under thirty.

All of us women listening to her nodded our heads quietly. We all sympathized with what she had to say. We all understood, every one of us, and the fact that we understood frightened me.

On Loneliness

It revealed the astonishing depths of our disillusionment. We fall in love, live with our lover, and gradually accumulate grudges and disappointments. Gradually we—fall out of love? No. We revise our concepts of love. We decide it wasn't love in the first place. We dissect the cadaver of our love and dreams and, since by now the entire corpse is already infested, the entire dream rotted, we decide the disease was terminal from the beginning. We analyze ourselves into a state of loneliness more profound than anything we experience living alone, for now we see the heights of the promise from the depths of our despair. We feel vaguely betrayed, as if we sacrificed our integrity for security and a warm bed.

When my marriage was falling apart, I became astonishingly productive: We moved into a larger apartment, bought furniture. I made drapes, painted, plastered. But when it was all done and I had to rest, I found that no number of rooms was enough to hold the bitterness.

Why do so many people who marry or live together end up disillusioned, lonely, and bitter? What creates and perpetuates that isolation in a double bed? Are we too spoiled to compromise or too unsure of what we want? Are we too sophisticated to settle for one of anything, even one person, even if it is one person at a time?

In personal relations, we learn to suppress our emotions, so that these emotions go underground and live a private life of their own. This is especially true when it involves those we are supposed to love. When we want to be left alone, or resent the intrusion on our privacy, when we are together and not connecting, when we are jabbing each other's sore spots—then the resentment and anger well up. Anger does have its place in love, and people who do not feel free to shout at one another may well be dependent on each other but are not likely to be intimate. There is a big difference between intimacy and dependency, which is why some people can begin and end a marriage feeling they never knew their partner—and, indeed, they never did.

As I suggested in Chapter Three, verbal battles are the salvation for many a healthy relationship, and some of the most volatile couples I know love each other best. Unfortunately, people try to be polite rather than honest. Feelings become so pent-up that people cannot even talk to each other anymore. This is so common that a marriage counseling technique has been developed in which romantic partners are taught how to reestablish communication by writing down their feelings in a notebook and then exchanging notebooks with a kiss.

Constant politeness at the dinner table is like constant politeness in bed. It gets boring. When we become polite is when the lies begin. "Sometimes it's as if husband and wife were making a long-distance call to one another on faulty telephones . . . sometimes it's the great silence of outer space," Johan tells his wife, Marianne, in Ingmar Bergman's film, *Scenes from a Marriage*. And the loneliness, he says, "hurts physically. It stings like a burn. Or like when you were little and had been crying and the whole inside of your body ached." The film shows the guilt behind disintegrating love.

After watching the movie, I saw one young woman in the row ahead of me alone and pregnant, crying quietly in her seat. I left the theater and stood by my bus stop, cold, shivering, and arms wrapped across my chest like a straitjacket. When I got home, I wrote my former husband a short note: "Please go see this movie." But he never did, and I understood that said a lot about what had been wrong with our marriage.

The thing about the film that struck home for me was that these two people were so pleasant to one another, and all the while resentments were infesting the marriage. Marianne tells her husband she thinks consideration killed their love, for they never quarreled despite the growing hate and disappointment. Johan looks at Marianne and says he was longing to smash "that white, hard resistance that radiated from you. But we chatted away so amicably to each other, joking about the nice times we had together in spite of everything."

This was much like my marriage, much like many marriages I have seen. It is not civil to get angry and shout and throw things. We act like eggs in fragile shells, afraid we will be easily broken.

Once upon a time, I knew two lovers much like Johan and Marianne. They had known each other for five years, and then they married. The man was gentle and kind, not too ambitious, and carried with him a quiet, solid air of reassurance. The woman was pretty enough and bright. She believed that only through marriage, and God knows she desperately wanted to be married, could she be happy. But she suspected, from what she heard from other women, that her husband would, somehow, disappoint her. He was to her both a salvation and a curse, a knight surrounded by a moat, and it turned out they did not know each other nearly as well as they had thought.

They set up housekeeping in the Midwest, and she decorated the apartment, became a gourmet cook, went to graduate school, and lobbied for the Equal Rights Amendment. He was a teacher and often worked evenings and weekends. While he watched sports on Sundays, she ironed his shirts, and once a month they went to visit one set of in-laws. Everyone said they were the perfect couple.

A slow and smoldering anger built up in her. She had thought that in marriage she would not be lonely anymore, but she felt lonely most of the time. Her anger ignited into larger and larger flames as her husband failed to live up to the image she had bestowed on him. She took a job in an office, and the job put her in daily contact with interesting people who admired her work. Her perceptions of herself changed, her confidence increased. After a few years, she began to feel she was leaving her husband behind, that she had married him to fill a need that was no longer there. But his needs were still there, still the same, and he wanted her to remain the same as the woman he first knew and loved. In her worst moments, he would pat and hold her while tears ran down her cheeks. They agreed that she was born to be unhappy.

A mental tug-of-war ensued. She and her husband clung to each other in panic, pulled apart, clung and pulled. They went to a marriage counselor, where they politely sat in adjacent chairs, nodding politely, each politely seeing the other's point of view. He watched a lot of television and she took long walks through the night. She thought about what marriage was supposed to be: growing closer together, sharing, building a home full of commitment and carpets, saving money, taking vacations to warm and welcoming places, having children, giving mutual support and encouragement, and, finally, serenely facing death while the children gather round—everything Louisa May Alcott ever promised.

She blamed herself, blamed her husband, blamed the institution of marriage for the terrible loneliness, hurt, and disappointment. The only kind of love she had known was the stifling love her mother gave her. Now she was trying to act out that same kind of love with her husband. She thought they should grow together like Siamese twins, that their hearts should beat as one. So why did love and marriage mix like water and hot grease, spattering and burning? She found it impossible to live with someone she cared about without being hurt or hurting him.

The husband desperately tried to keep communication open, remembering his own parents' thirty years of wedded silence and bored indifference. He felt hurt and mystified and betrayed. The sex was good, and that part of the daily routine was pleasant and reassuring. She made him feel good about himself, and the marriage gave his life a kind of hope and promise. He liked having her around at night; he even helped her cook occasionally.

She let the pain build up until, when it finally surfaced and exploded, the shrapnel hit friends, family, anyone in the way, wounding unintentionally all the wrong people and driving them away from her, reinforcing her loneliness. She envied those who could direct their anger at the proper target and then cool off, without having to scream it out on a psychologist's couch. On the surface, she had always been so nice, so pleasant to be with, so understanding. Now, learning to express anger was new and strange. She had to open up new circuits in the brain. It was like learning to use an atrophied limb.

On their last night together, the husband tried to make the wife stay, and she knelt, weeping and screaming, on the kitchen floor. Only the sound of her screams, she thought later, kept her in touch with a last shred of sanity, with the core of herself she was trying to save. She left that night and now lives alone and far away. The husband has found another woman to live with him.

I, too, had a pleasant marriage to a kind and gentle man. It lasted four years, and by the time it was over, we had smothered our love under a suffocating blanket of romanticism.

Toward the end of my marriage, I visited my friend Kathy M. in the nearby spacious apartment she shared with her husband. She was worried because I had become so quiet the last few months. We sat at the kitchen table, and I listened to the coffee dribble through the filter into the white Melitta pot. I thought: *If I can keep in touch with this, with textures and smells, if I can water my plants and take the bus to work each morning, then I will be all right even though my marriage is disintegrating, even though something is going dead inside.* I seemed to have developed a permanent-press pleat between my eyes.

Kathy M. and I talked about our husbands. Her marriage was equally shaky but for reasons very different from mine. She talked about the weeks without making love, the months without real conversation, the years without affection. Her husband was as calculating as an adding machine. I sometimes watched him pacing back and forth through their apartment, reading the stock market reports, going to his club for a swim. I saw him with male friends, saw the hail-fellow-well-met heartiness, the joking and bluffing that said: Don't get too close, I don't want you to know how I really am, how confused, how weak, how lonely. I saw him with Kathy—sometimes talking in a clipped voice, sometimes domineering and smug, sometimes childlike as he opened up a bottle of fine wine. ("That's his way of telling me he wants sex tonight," she said.) He was eager to please in the only ways emotionally open to him.

Years later I came across a book on male depression called *I Don't Want To Talk About It* in which the author, psychotherapist Terence Real, describes one of his patients who reminded me of Kathy M.'s husband. He grew up in a family with parents who rarely demonstrated physical affection with each other and stopped showing him affection when he was about six years old. It wasn't until his MBA graduation when he was twenty-six years old that his father hugged him and said he loved him for the first time in his life. Real went on to say that "withholding any expression of love until a young boy is a grown man is a form of emotional violence and . . . the violence men level against themselves and others is bred from just such circumstances."

I wondered which horror is greater: Kathy M. living with icy polite control, which could be a form of passive violence, or my life with XX and being engulfed by too much failed romanticism. Of course, at this point in my marriage, my emotions were swinging back and forth like a metronome, going from one extreme to the other in a frantic attempt to find a combination of release and control that worked, that could save us. Kathy M. did the same thing: She and her husband would have brief romantic interludes on his signal, and then slip back into silence. But nothing worked for long—for either of us. Kathy talked about the money her husband made, the vacations they took to Spain, Africa, South America. "In two months' time," she said, "I will have saved $7,400 of my own money, and maybe then I will leave him." The two months came and went, once, twice. She stayed, and she told me she often wakes in the night and goes into the living room and weeps.

Her inability to halt this slow self-destruction reminds me of the love rites of the praying mantis. During mating season the male praying mantis mounts the female to perform a ritual that will destroy him: As he holds her in his firm embrace she slowly chews off his head. Still, out of passion, instinct, or foolishness, he hangs on until the job is done. We humans will also let someone eat us alive in the name of what we call love.

Sometimes the very routine of living together seems to kill love and make people feel hollow: It is the cleaning and cooking and long working hours; the accumulation of petty frustrations and repetitions; deciding what to eat for dinner; socks on the floor; second or third drinks at dinner which provide an excuse for nonconversation and early sleep; Saturday nights in front of the television. It is the neat pile of politeness and obligations that finally kill the spontaneity and joy and begin to numb you and make love go stale.

One Saturday morning in the paneled family room of a comfortable New York suburb home, I had coffee with a couple whose unhappy marriage was ordinary enough to be a cliché. She took me aside and told me: "It's as if my husband and I each live in the same house alone. I used to think we were an ideal couple. I can't put my finger on what happened. It's just that as the years started passing, Ed did a lot of traveling for his job, and I immersed myself in the house and kids. I dread Sundays. In the summer he's in the backyard or basement and I'm in the family room or kitchen. Even in the winter, we don't talk—we now avoid being in the same room together. When he comes home after a rough day at the office, he doesn't confide in me. Sometimes I make love to him when he asks me to but when I say yes and mean no I feel like a prostitute. I want other people to like me, but I don't really know whether my husband likes me or not. I don't know what he thinks of me. I just don't want him to leave me."

Later on, the husband and I talked in his den. "We've reached the point where we can go to the same party, sit in the same room, and be totally apart. We're each wrapped up in our separate lives. As time goes on, I'm spending more time at work. It doesn't seem to matter because when I'm home, I just watch television to not be put on the carpet and questioned. I can sit there in my shell, let my mind wander. I feel like I'm in one corner making money, and these other four people—my wife and kids—are running around in the other corner spending it. Sometimes during sex, I get the impression she thinks she's doing me a favor. But when she says no to sex I get upset and sulk. I know she feels hurt when I do that, but I wonder why she is rejecting me—am I losing my sexual attraction? I feel lonely most of the time and I don't even know why."

Another couple I know has suffered through thirty years of married martyrdom. They rarely speak to one another anymore, except to bicker. On their twenty-fifth wedding anniversary, friends threw them a party. After they cut the cake, they posed for pictures. The photographer asked the husband to put his arm around his wife. "Give her a kiss!" he shouted. When the husband obligingly pecked his wife on the cheek, she flinched.

"When people in miserable marriages say: 'I'd rather stay married than be alone,' what they really mean is: 'Anger gives me an opportunity to stay alive,'" a marriage counselor told me. "They mean: 'If I didn't have this person to fight with or fend off, I would feel dead, which is worse than loneliness.' They need someone to fuel their emotions. This is one of the reasons why people get married and stay married, or go from one marriage to another—and are lonely even while doing it."

One psychologist I know (researching this book, I got to know a lot of therapists) has been married four times. He considers living alone to be a dreadful disease. His mother was seldom home when he was young, and his sister, whom he was close to, died when he was seven.

"Classical psychology says if you're a big boy, you can make it on your own. I say if you're a big boy, you're smart enough to have someone by your side," he says. "My mother can't understand why I have been divorced and remarried so many times. She and my father have been married thirty-nine years. Of course, their marriage totally destroyed her. She's a college graduate but is almost illiterate now. She hasn't read a newspaper for twenty years. She's always depressed. My father complains he has no one to talk to because his wife is a vegetable.

"I want more out of marriage," he continued, "but my wives and I seem to fall into the same roles my parents did. It's hard to ignore all those years of conditioning. It's strange that even with all my training in psychology, I still make the same mistakes as everybody else. Each of my wives has been intelligent, but when we marry, our love seems to turn into a struggle for power, for supremacy. I end up the winner who's won nothing—no mothering, no loving, no sex."

It is not chic to talk about love and power in the same breath. Power seems to have more to do with territory, security, and expectations than it does with loving. But it crops up every time we feel threatened, and nothing threatens us more than love. When we love someone, we become vulnerable to them. Vulnerability makes us uneasy and so we set up defenses and manipulations to protect ourselves.

When we fall in love, each of us wants to control it so we won't get hurt. As soon as we try to control love, it slips away from us. The power plays we use to protect our love end up destroying it.

I know people who feel so vulnerable in love that they put up a front. They jockey to hold power over the other person, and struggle to keep from being committed. They fail to see that in love their weaknesses can be complemented by someone else's strengths, and that their strengths can complement someone else's weaknesses. They have not learned to handle the delicate process of love in which mutual needs are recognized and supported. As a result, they are lonely, for they have a hard time finding a love that survives.

Gone with the Wind is a classic example of how these power plays are used in love.* Concealed beneath what appears to be a romantic and tragic love story is one of the most power-hungry love affairs ever filmed. Yet, despite the cunning and manipulation portrayed in the film, decades of girls and boys dreamed wistfully about Scarlett O'Hara and Rhett Butler's great romance. They were a prototype that two generations of women and men have used as their models for how to act in love.

In the beginning, Scarlett and Rhett admire each other for their independence and spunk. As the land and culture of the Old South are destroyed by Civil War, they begin the slow process of

---

* Within the context of the book I focus here on damaging romantic stereotypes portrayed in *Gone with the Wind*. However, it is also one of the most racist films ever produced, one that denies the brutalities of slavery and perpetuates racist stereotypes. Black Americans have protested its showings in theaters since its opening in 1939 and, most recently, its release on a streaming service in 2020.

destroying each other in the name of love. Rhett loves Scarlett because she represents all he admires. She is an opportunist like him. But Rhett's love is tragic and unfulfilled, for Scarlett is hopelessly in love with Ashley Wilkes—and that is what eventually destroys her.

She marries Rhett because she needs his money and strength and wants the status of being a married woman—and she intends to give nothing in return. Alll the while she is married to Rhett, she plots to catch Ashley. Once Ashley is attainable, in the true romantic tradition, he ceases being her ideal. Then Scarlett falls in love with her husband who no longer gives a damn about her. The way all this is packaged makes love seem heroic, tragic, and marvelous. It makes us sympathetic to the sadomasochism that comes out of need and fear, and to the insidious manipulations used in place of love.

Gone With The Wind made women feel they could manipulate men by appearing coy and childlike. The film made men feel they could manipulate women with a swashbuckling, devil-may-care attitude that thinly concealed sexual prowess. It was a formula for controlling the opposite sex. Rhett and Scarlett were realists and amoral people who would do anything to get what they wanted. Scarlett would willingly betray any woman for a man. She marries for convenience, not love. In the end, her desire for power leaves her isolated, lonely, and deserted by both Rhett and Ashley, the men she tried so desperately to control.

Rhett oozes power. In the Civil War, he plays both ends against the middle. He tries to control Scarlett through his wealth, sex, and their child. He is a chameleon—he blends in with his surroundings, and his elusiveness gives him power. When he marries Scarlett, he stops being "rowdy" and instead becomes "respectable" so he can get recognition and acceptance for both of them and their daughter. He is the fraternity man, the ambitious corporate executive one hundred years before his time. But it is the flirtatious Scarlett, with her eighteen-inch waist, who is the true villain, playing deadly games with people's hearts.

I didn't realize all this when I saw *Gone with the Wind* as a child. I forgot that Scarlett said, "Why does a girl have to be so silly (i.e., flirtatious and coy) to catch a husband?" and how Rhett manipulated Scarlett's frustrations by pretending that she couldn't hurt him. I forgot Scarlett's ability to exploit his love. I was too young to see the conundrum of her personality: split between the need to control the man who tries to love her and her attraction to an unavailable man. The hoop skirt and sabers are gone, but love affairs like Rhett and Scarlett's linger on, held together by illusions and hidden, desperate needs.

To this day, the Scarlett O'Hara kind of woman persists . . . soft and pretty but with the exterior covering a need to dominate. Because she had spunk and guts, she was a survivor, and audiences back then admired her for that but failed to see the destructive power behind her beauty and spirit.

Scarlett murders love with the same deft hand she murders the Union soldier, and both times makes the same glib reflection that she will think about it tomorrow. But, of course, she will never really think about it, any more than many people today think about how they murder love by trying to manipulate it. With their destruction of love, they are truly alone and powerless.

In Rhett and Scarlett's day, the question of sexual fidelity was never openly discussed. It is different today. For many, and certainly for me, fidelity has become the thorniest part of love. Nothing disturbs me more than the thought that my lover could be sleeping with someone else.

Most people I know try to be reasonable about infidelity. They tell themselves it's only sex, after all, and it doesn't affect the foundation of their love. It isn't the end of the world. I know one couple who, after twenty years of marriage, finally agreed they could each have sex with other people and they would only tell the other about it if they felt the affair was getting "serious." This way, they reasoned, they wouldn't argue over unimportant sexual forays.

I listened to them talk about it. They called it "dialog" and they were very understanding with each other. It suddenly flashed through my mind that these two people were being so polite to one another because they did not love each other anymore. I thought: Even if the love is gone, they must want the marriage to work. Then I realized they may well love each other; how was I to judge? My reaction was just my own prejudice operating. To me, lovers who show no sexual jealousy are emotional foreigners.

"My husband and I have a built-in conflict," a friend told me. "Neither of us just jumps into bed with people, so we aren't concerned about fidelity most of the time. But when we sleep with someone, it is usually for something more than just the sex; it usually involves deeper emotions, and so it is always a threat to both of us." I have seen a wife sit at her kitchen table and say she considers fidelity the bedrock of her marriage, while the husband sat at the other end of the table, silent and staring straight ahead.

Am I faithful if I sleep only with my partner, but in doing so must close my eyes and pretend he is someone else? Am I faithless if I take another lover, knowing that because he is around I can better cope with my marriage? Am I faithful to myself if I sleep with a man I barely care about? Is there value in the experience itself, or am I selling out? What does genital sex have to do with emotional fidelity?

"If you have a good thing going with someone, you're not going to leave because you find someone else with a penis two inches longer or an IQ twenty points higher," one man told me. That's certainly true. But it makes the dilemma no less confusing.

Erik Erikson says "diversity and fidelity are polarized. They make each other significant and keep each other alive. Fidelity without a sense of diversity can become an obsession and a bore; diversity without fidelity, an empty relativism." I suppose I have been needlessly faithful and carelessly unfaithful. Loneliness makes us reach out for comforting arms, sometimes with unwise people in unwise places.

One woman I know seems to have resolved it all. She tells me: "The more secure I get about myself, the more secure I get about him. I know he enjoys being what he is when he's with me, and I enjoy what he gives me. There may be several women he sleeps with who I don't know about. I don't want to know and he wouldn't tell me if I asked, and I'm glad because we would only waste a lot of time discussing my insecurities. This way, we really have a terrific time when we're together." This woman is the wisest person I know, and I believe her, but I would still like to see her alone in her bed on a night when he doesn't show up.

The problem with infidelity is that it sometimes makes us feel guilty. When we feel guilty, it ends up infecting all areas of the relationship and makes us want to confess all to relieve our burden.

I have noticed, however, that people who truly love each other do not treat love like a report card. They do not tell each other everything. I have met wounded and lonely people in many "open" marriages. The litany is: "John and I don't keep any secrets. We believe things shouldn't be kept hidden. We just lay it out in the open so we can deal with it."

Truth, like sanity, can be a very fragile thing. People who make this kind of confession often do so because they want to hurt someone rather than clear the air and salvage the love. Often, it is an excuse to dump their guilt. Neither case has anything to do with openness between two equals but has a great deal to do with loneliness à deux.

On Loneliness

An article on divorce in *New York Magazine* in the 1970s blamed much of our love problems on psychotherapy and feminism: "Thanks to psychotherapy, dependency is a double felony—you're a cripple and your mate has got you around his neck . . . No one wants to settle or accommodate . . . Everyone wants more . . . To grow means to grow apart." About women, it said: "Suddenly, no one wants to be the wife. Movement women, it is rumored, are prime carriers and can transmit divorce fever over the phone."

The message I get is that the divorce rate is rising because we are becoming narcissists—everybody is out for themselves. One divorcée in the article said of her marriage: "Life is always a compromise, but I thought I could get a better compromise."

These attitudes are convenient, but they don't get to the root of the dilemma. Everything was in flux in the 1970s and still is—people are seeking new and broader definitions of love. Divorce statistics don't tell us what is going on. They just tell us that something is going on. There are many ways of loving, and we are only beginning to see that the ways that count most are complicated and intricate, without formula, without guidelines, and based on good instincts rather than old clichés. People are still willing to compromise to make love work, but they are not willing to play the games their parents played.

Now we are beginning to see that the "ideal" marriage, the fantasy "forever" love à la Duke and Duchess of Windsor, cannot be obtained without sacrificing some personal identity along the way. Many people no longer want to do this, to live in the shadow of another person. Philip Slater says that the "mystical, spiritualized, idealized" feelings that go along with this kind of married love have incestuous undertones.

By believing that only one person can satisfy us emotionally and sexually, understand us, take care of us, live with us and for us, and fill all our needs, we are asking for a surrogate parent. And, as a result, we are guaranteed to be short on sex and long on loneliness, broken hearts and homes, and therapy bills. When we idealize our spouses, our family lives are bound to end in bitterness. As Ernest Becker says, when we live with a lover every day, "we see that our gods have clay feet."

Today, we have more distractions, more worries, more mobility, and fewer children than any previous generation, all of which are magnified by the media. The pace of our lives has quickened. The possibilities and temptations of the world flood into our homes, bedrooms, cars every second. We are not as easy to please; we become restless. We were reared with the idea of change and built-in obsolescence—in our clothing, our appliances, and, unfortunately, our loves. We tend to get easily bored; it's as simple as that. In practical terms, we don't need marriage as we once knew it anymore, even though emotionally we may want it.

The women's movement of the 1960s and 1970s began to give women the courage to leave what would otherwise have lingered on as bad and often destructive relationships. Today, women know they can find a network of support no matter where they live—in a town, suburb, city, even rural area—no matter how isolated they feel emotionally and physically. But I don't think more marriages are bad because of women's liberation; I think people are just quicker to end bad marriages that in our grandparents' time would have survived fifty winters while the ice gradually hardened their hearts.

Women have in the past often felt passive and out of control in their relations with men. This is why, when I have heard women say they "hate men," I often suspect they mean that they hate the way they react to men, for it is their reaction—their sense of being submissive and helpless—rather than the man himself that destroys them.

On Loneliness

Many heterosexual women feel elated when they finally recognize the importance of their own needs and no longer subjugate them to their partners' needs. I felt great when, for the first time, I ignored my husband's request to stay home and flew out to Wounded Knee to cover the uprising of Native Americans for a newspaper. I found I was greeted on my return with new respect that indicated to both of us that I had at last tapped an internal reservoir of self-confidence that would irrevocably change the nature of our marriage.

In the best of relationships, people give each other time and space to be themselves, to have privacy, to be alone. They do not share everything. They allow for different approaches to living, especially in the "small" things that can accumulate until they destroy love. One woman I know never goes to parties at the same time as her husband. He likes to go early and not stay late. She likes to arrive late and leave with the last guests. "We made an arrangement, and we stuck to it. It worked out fine for twenty years," she says. "Because of compromises like this, I found a lot of freedom in my marriage. My marriage is a bedrock that has left me free to pursue interests I wouldn't pursue otherwise. Sometimes the more clear our commitments are, the more freedom we have."

Another friend hasn't gone shopping with his wife for ten years because he likes to run into the store, choose fast, and get out, but his wife will take an hour to buy a toothbrush. "By not shopping together, we reduced friction in matters where there are no rights and wrongs," he says. "Once we realized our rhythms didn't match, we stayed away from that situation. We've learned from watching our friends. They get confused over who picks out the clothes, who buys the furniture. The husband can't make a decision and so he palms it off on his wife and then blames her when he disagrees with the choice. Trouble begins when you feel you're responsible for the other person. That's when the resentment builds up."

One secret of constructive love is learning not to cling, not to control, not to demand. Clingers almost always get left. I know a clinging woman whose husbands, all three of them, left her without a word of goodbye. She claimed in each case that she had had no idea anything was wrong. People cling not only to romantic myths but to the habits of their parents, to their neuroses and needs. None of it works in love.

Clingers are afraid, and out of fear they sometimes compromise themselves out of existence. I recently heard a woman talk about her husband and the sacrifices she had made. In twenty-one years of marriage, she had reduced herself to a cipher, living only through her husband. "He always says things like: 'There's a pimple on your chin, do something about it; there's a hair out of place, fix it,'" she said. "When we're going out he'll say: 'Nope, I don't like that dress, change it.' He's told me if I were fat and ugly he would leave me. He has made me unbelievably vain, and for the most part I accommodate. His attitude is: When I take my wife someplace, I want men to look at her. That's why I'm so hung up on getting older."

In a good relationship, you value yourself every bit as much as the person you love. This does not mean there is no compromise. There is always a delicate and shifting balance between fostering who you are and taking care of the needs of the other person. One psychiatrist gave me his formula for keeping love intact through the years. He told me, in effect, that you handle love like a business. It may sound cold and cynical, but what he meant was that each person respects the other's integrity, which is surely the kindest way to treat someone. It means both partners work at love every day, just as you would work at a business that you take pride in and want to pass on to your children. You don't ignore a business, or downgrade it, or leave it untended for weeks at a time, he explained. Yet people do this to their love without a second thought. It takes little energy to plod through life and love. But it takes active participation to enjoy living and loving.

Ari Kiev, former director of the Social Psychiatry Research Institute in New York, said he thinks that love should be handled like a sport. "When you live with somebody, you've got to think of them as being on the other side of the court," he said. "It's like tennis or skiing. When you ski, you ski alone on your own skis even when you are with someone. You ski together, yes, but separately. It's the same with love. The problem is that we know how to seduce a lover but we don't know how to leave and then come back. We don't have enough confidence that the divine spark that made love happen in the first place will be there again. And, inevitably, as soon as we consciously try to preserve it, we lose it. When we lose that sense of ourselves as separate and whole, then we fall flat on our face."

"However close people get," he continued, "they can't feel that close all the time. They make love. Then the guy says: 'Gee, it's later than I thought.' And she says: 'You don't love me' and he says: 'No, I love you. I won't go right away.' People set up rituals, ceremonial ways of communicating, and they become insincere and lonely."

What I care about is finding the best ways of loving myself so I can find the best way of loving someone else. I have been in love, and been hurt; I have been married, and the marriage has failed. I would do it all again. Someday I will find a healthy kind of loving, and when I do, it will be so natural that I will forget I was ever looking for it.

7

Friends

"What makes loneliness an anguish is not that I have no one to share my burden; But this: I have only my own burden to bear."
(*Dag Hammarskjöld,* Markings)

So far, I have been more successful at loving friends than lovers. My friends and I understand that it is all right to not share everything and keep some mysteries and surprises to ourselves. We know it is all right sometimes to feel lonely even while we are with one another, that we cannot satisfy all of one another's needs. My lovers and I, on the other hand, too often turn away from the world and circle into ourselves, creating a closed system. With no input from the outside world, the relationship soon goes stale and dries up like a lake with no fresh water flowing through.

My friendships last longer because they are less possessive, more realistic, and more flexible. I don't demand as much from friends as I do from lovers, and as a result, I usually get more than I expected. When my friendships do end, they fade away painlessly (for the most part) while my endings with lovers are more traumatic, with one of us ready to twist the knife one last time before we part.

On Loneliness

Unlike my lovers, who I try to mold into a form to fit my illusions, I find each friendship is as unique as the people in it. I have social friends, for example, who I like to go with to a concert, on a bike ride, or for a drink. But my social friends are not always the people I can talk with best. We may know each other for years and not grow any closer, and yet the friendship works all right for both of us. My social friends tend to be people I've worked with or gone to school with. Such friendships are often convenient and sometimes pay off in unexpected ways.

It is nice, for example, to have a friend with a house in the country who extends an open-ended invitation. It helps to be friends with your doctor—who might just handle your medical problem on a weekend or holiday. There is nothing wrong with this kind of relationship, as long as both people respect and appreciate its limits.

But those of us who have a lot of friends can still be lonely if all the friendships stay on this level, especially if we are never sure who values us for who we are, and who values us for what we do or have. Social friendships are often a bandage solution for our loneliness and fall by the wayside when we move, change jobs, or drop out of a club.

Intimate friendships are something entirely different. They involve a lot of work and attention, and most people are lucky if they know one or two people they can call best friends—soul friends, people you cherish, people you would protect, shelter, and do anything for. Intimate friendship involves sacrifice and compromise and responsibility. It involves staying in touch even when you're "too busy," and caring about another person to the point where you will, without a second thought, go out of your way to help.

Some people are never able to develop such a friendship. I find this especially true of some men who are unable to get beyond the clubby rah-rah type of friendship that their fathers knew. A novel called *Steppenwolf*, published in the 1920s, best describes this kind of man: ". . . a great many people liked him, but it was no more than sympathy and friendliness. . . for the air of lonely men surrounded him. . . a still atmosphere in which the world around him slipped away, leaving him incapable of relationship."

"I've gone through different schools of therapy and couch-sitting, but none of them taught me how to become close to people, how to make friends," one man told me. "Feeling warmth with people is like swimming: You either know how to do it, or you don't. I grew up afraid of my real feelings, and anything I feel now must penetrate a thick layer of fear."

This man buys things as substitutes for friends. "I look at an object and I say: 'Okay, that will give me pleasure,' and I get it and then find out that I'm bored with it. I treat people the same way, but I purchase them with 'mind games' rather than with money. The truth is I feel closed to people I meet and to my relatives and to the lady I go to bed with. I create an aura of callousness to buffer my fear, but I think any real feelings I once had have probably shriveled up by now."

If you are incapable of opening up, unable to trust, give, or share, if you are defensive and evasive, then you will feel friendless and lonely. For a long while, I certainly did. Early friendships fell by the wayside, one after the other. I never knew what happened. I thought something was wrong with all of my alleged friends when in fact it was me all along who had trouble caring and reaching out. Until you value yourself, you cannot value your friends. Until you know that you are the most important person in your life, you cannot let anyone else become important to you without feeling threatened by it. For a long time, I did not value myself.

I realized this one afternoon after spending an especially depressing day alone with myself and my computer. Exhausted by my battles with both, I finally gave up and went to the corner bar, the White Horse Tavern, to have a beer. In the past, when I went there alone, I was always armed with a newspaper or book to prevent people (especially men) from approaching me. But this time I took nothing to read; I had just my misery for company. I ordered a beer and looked around. I suddenly realized how foolish my need for weapons had been and that no one could threaten me because I was my own worst enemy.

I often complained about "being hassled" in bars and on the street, but all at once I understood that I did not need to be a passive victim but could, in fact, be very much in control of myself and others if I chose to. Instead of sinking into my protective huddle, I sat up, looked around, and began to talk, to really *be* with people in that bar for the first time. My ego was not at stake; I felt I had nothing to lose. I did not care if people liked me, but I was interested in finding out about them, if for no other reason than to stop thinking about my troubles and to break out of my loneliness. It was as if I had wandered from under a dark cloud into the sunlight. The bar opened up to me. I found interesting, kind people all around and talked to those I wanted to. I could feel the atmosphere change because of my self-assurance and air of independence.

I learned a valuable lesson that day. Often, I feel people threaten me, and I become closed and defensive. My own petty problems assume enormous proportions. And when you think about yourself too much, as Don Juan says, "It gives you a strange fatigue that makes you shut off the world around you and cling to your arguments."

Lonely people feel friendless, and often are, if they are unable to forget themselves long enough to really care about someone else. There are other excuses I like to use to keep people away. Sometimes I close up because I feel like a victim, as if other people were manipulating me, and this makes me withdraw and feel sorry for myself. Sometimes I feel intimidated; certain that I am not smart enough or beautiful enough, I cover up my insecurities by hiding the "real me" under what I hope is a more acceptable social mask.

We alienate ourselves from people when we feed off our misery, when we fail to take total responsibility for ourselves, when we cannot accept ourselves the way we are. We feel lonely when we become dishonest, when we play games to protect ourselves. Even if we hide behind a pleasant facade, people will avoid us, because no matter what words our lips are forming, we are telling them to leave us alone.

We often hide behind other excuses—liquor, or drugs, or children, or a spouse—to keep people away. I have a friend who has five dogs in his city apartment. The dogs are smelly, noisy, and time-consuming and, as he has become more preoccupied with them, fewer people come to visit. The dogs began as a substitute for people, but they have ended up perpetuating this man's loneliness. They are his wall against people.

I also have a friend who hangs a small flag at her window when she doesn't want visitors. In this way, she controls who enters her life, but she does it in such an arbitrary and hostile way that she has few friends. After all, who wants friendship conducted like a traffic light? Her next-door neighbor, on the other hand, always has extra food or coffee for an unexpected guest. She welcomes people into her life (though she also protects her privacy when she has to) and as a result, she has many friends.

But we don't need special excuses to tell people how we feel. Our body language, the tone of our voice, the way we avoid looking in a person's eyes—all are dead giveaways when we feel uncomfortable around people. We are, all of us, much more sensitive to body language and silent messages than we give ourselves credit for. We know that it doesn't take a psychic to feel the difference between, say, a heavy silence and a comfortable silence. We know that "bad vibes" are something we can sense; it's as if the airwaves themselves are hostile.

I found this out for myself one day when I ate lunch with a former addict in the lunchroom of a drug rehabilitation center. During the meal, I had the feeling I had been there before. So many things seemed familiar—the atmosphere, the aura, something I couldn't quite put my finger on. Yet, as far as I knew, I had never been in a similar situation. That night I realized that it was the same atmosphere I felt in my weekly karate class—the controlled violence, sensitive tension, quiet sustained watchfulness, the wariness. My conscious mind didn't connect the two, but the similarity was so strong that my subconscious picked it up immediately. In the same way, subconscious messages keep people from us.

Some of this apprehension about others, especially strangers, is a gut-level animal response, a fight-or-flight reaction that is leftover from prehistoric days. Our adrenaline flows, our heart beats, we get ready to defend ourselves even though today such a response can do us more harm than good. Even the origin of shaking hands was to display the fact that you were not carrying a weapon.

"Back in the days when all men went armed with a sword or similar weapons, there was always a crucial moment when strangers met," Jean Rosenbaum explains in his book, *Is Your Volkswagen a Sex Symbol?* "The question had to be answered quickly: Was this to be a peaceful meeting or a violent one? If peace was the intent, both men either laid down their weapons or did not draw them. They approached each other with outstretched, empty hands, and to further ensure against possible trickery, each man took the right hand of the other to prevent him from changing his mind and drawing his weapon."

Friends

Bertrand Russell has also pointed this out: "The natural instinct of man . . . is to investigate every stranger of his species with a view to deciding whether he is friendly or hostile . . . this instinct is inhibited by those who travel in the subway in rush hour. The result is a generally diffuse rage against all the strangers brought into involuntary contact."

At a party, we all become actresses and actors. We walk around with our guard up, locked behind our smiles. I am always lonely in a crowd because I think everyone notices my faults, sees through my façade. It's as if all my flaws were multiplied by the number of people there. Erik Erikson calls this reaction "simultaneous reflection and observation."

For example, a woman at a party will see other people looking at her and wonder how she looks to them. This is her reflection. But she, in turn, is observing. She is judging, weighing, deciding that she doesn't like this person and could like that one. People who do this all the time find it very hard to make friends with people. They tend to dismiss people and stereotype them. Most of us react this way to some degree when we are in social situations, and the extent to which we do it determines how much we feel threatened, uneasy, and lonely.

Some people cover up their uneasiness by being a clown, or a bully, or a loudmouth—anything that works for them, that controls the way they relate to people and the way they let people relate to them. They may boast, gossip, giggle, or tell long windy stories. Their constant motion and noise are protection. No one can catch them. Other people hide under the cover of social superiority. They are dandies or princesses; they want to be fussed over. The tactics differ, but the message is the same: They are afraid of not being liked, afraid of being judged, afraid of being found out.

For a long time, I would walk into a room filled with people and go to an empty corner or isolated chair and sit there alone. I wanted people to come to me and didn't want to go to them. I suspect one reason I went into journalism was that, by representing a newspaper, I had immediate stature; I could meet people without being committed in any way.

Then one day in group therapy, I was asked to stand up and talk about how I felt about myself. It was terrifying. My throat tightened as if a cotton ball had lodged there, my knees shook, my face flushed. It was the first time in my life I realized to what extent I hid in corners, how frightened I was of being exposed and vulnerable. After it was over, I felt tremendous relief. I felt I had revealed my worst secrets and discovered to my surprise that the people there still liked me. In fact, they liked me better than they did before.

We all want to be liked by some people, but most of us want to be liked by too many people. I have an ingratiating smile, a habit I developed from a lifetime of trying to placate and be nice. The smile flashes messages: Love me; I am charming; I am witty. That smile has cost me a lot. I feel like the guy in Joseph Heller's *Catch-22* "who wanted only to be liked, and was destined to be disappointed in even so humble and degrading an ambition."

We think if we have more friends we will be less lonely, but this isn't true if friendships are based only on pleasantries. We cannot be all things to all people. To always be nice to everyone we know is dishonest; it prevents us from becoming an intimate friend—or having one. Hoping to be liked, always fearing rejection, is a losing game.

It takes no effort to just be with people and be open to them. The effort comes when we keep them at arm's length and keep our guard up. It comes when we pass judgment, when we impose expectations, when we try to change people. As Nietzsche says, "A man as he ought to be: that sounds to us as insipid as a 'tree as it ought to be.'" We need be no more than we are.

Friends

I felt uneasy among other people because I could not face and accept who I was or who they were. Instead of accepting people, I became righteous: I criticized and scorned. I manipulated people by trying to make them fit my needs and dreams. Because of this, I had few friends.

One of the first was a reporter at the newspaper where I worked. We went to lunch and had drinks together. We talked about books, politics, and porcelain. She was outgoing and made friends easily. Early one morning she called to say she was leaving on an out-of-town assignment. She suggested I come along to write a magazine version of the story while she filed daily reports. I hesitated, but her enthusiasm was contagious. I packed my bags and went, and the story I produced ended up on the cover of a major magazine. Without her encouragement, I would have been intimidated by such a venture. We shared a sense of adventure and curiosity that made both of our lives more exciting.

She built up my ego, made me feel valuable. She admired me, trusted me, confided in me. She finally broke through what Alvarez calls "the frozen sea within us." We put a lot of work into that friendship, and, although we now live in separate cities, and have for several years, it still survives, still bound together by phone calls, Zoom, mutual support, and the sparks that we generate off each other. She taught me that one has to learn to be a friend, that the ability to develop intimate friendships is not always a natural, spontaneous act between people but is rather an art that takes work, care, and attention.

Friendship is an exchange of time, emotional support, and confidences—depending on its nature. Those who try to never ask for anything because they feel unworthy can never form real friendships. Those who are overly generous are often buying friendship because they are desperate to be liked.

Gift-giving—that is, the exchange of material gifts—is often a good clue to the way a person relates to others. I had a hard time learning to give and to receive. Other people I know have trouble with it too. Some people give things to cover up the fact that they are not giving anything of themselves. Other people hate to give gifts because they are afraid the gift, and they, will be rejected. Some people find it just as hard to receive a gift. I know a woman who can't handle her birthday because she feels every gift implies an obligation to do something in return. Also, she cannot believe that someone would give her a present simply because she was liked.

In good friendships, we can give the things we own, or the money we have, as long as we value the friend more than what we are giving away. We can give with ease, with warmth and love, as long as we are sure of our priorities, as long as we know how much we can give away without resenting it. My rule of thumb is: If you think you might be sorry later, don't give it—whether it's advice, sympathy, or something wrapped in tissue paper. When I give away too much, it compromises me, degrades the other person, and threatens the foundation of our friendship.

Even the best of friends keep certain things for themselves. Good friends, like good lovers, respect each other's privacy. They don't intrude. They know the importance of distance as well as sharing, and that the things that make us different from one another are as significant as the things we have in common.

Late one evening while I was spending a weekend at a friend's house, her phone rang. She spoke softly into the phone and said she would call back later. At 2:00 a.m., just as I was falling asleep, I heard her return the call. The next morning I wanted to ask whom she had called. I suspected it was a former lover who I thought wasn't good for her. But I knew it wasn't any of my business. She didn't tell me who called, and I never asked. If she wanted to tell me, she would in her own good time. As Harry Guntrip says: "In a good relationship, one knows how to wait."

Of course, my friendships have their ups and downs. Each one seems to have a cycle and a character all its own. Each goes through changes and metamorphoses; each is unique as a work of art.

I sometimes feel like my friends and I are playing a game in which two people face each other, clasp hands, and then pull each other around the room in circles, each taking turns tugging at the other. When I need help, my friends take the lead: give advice, criticize, admonish, encourage. When they need help, I seem miraculously together, and I take the lead. We take turns supporting each other. Sometimes my friendships stop and start again, feel distant and then close. Sometimes I despair and think the friendship is over: It founders and we seem to be going our separate ways—but then, somehow, we come back together again.

All in all, my friendships are the bedrock of my life, the deep current that carries me past obstacles and depression. They are my life-support system; I use them for survival. I hold friends in my heart like a precious jewel in my hand. Last fall, I stood with a friend watching a big-bellied freighter slide down the Hudson River, emptied of its cargo and heading back to sea. Its red underside was high above the waterline. Swallows encircled it in a twilight sky. A train going north hooted once in passing and the freighter hooted back. From the distant bluffs came the echoes of their greetings. I felt a shiver go up my spine. My life seemed contained in that instant with the continuity of the river, the brief encounter of the train and ship, and the closeness of my friend. We were silent. We stood together and yet I felt unique and alone, felt the weight, substance, and richness of my separateness. Dag Hammarskjöld wrote that "friendship needs no words—it is solitude delivered from the anguish of loneliness." That was how I felt at that instant. Finally, my friend turned to me. "Life is too short," she said, guessing all. We both knew, without ever saying so, that we had shared a special moment, between friends.

One of the assumptions I lived with is that my friends in college and at my jobs would be my friends forever. Yet, there are so many friends I have left by the wayside. In college we talked for hours. Six years later, I could hardly fill thirty seconds of conversation when I dropped in on a former classmate who lived near my parents. She had married out of college, had children. My friend looked worn out, unkempt, harassed. I started to tell her about my work and travels but stopped when I saw the envy in her eyes. I felt ashamed and realized how insensitive it was of me to come unannounced. She seemed to be trapped, so isolated, so different from who she had once been.

I was not interested, really, in her children's sleeping habits and teething. We had been friends because I was interested in *her*, but the *her* seemed to have disappeared. She had become like the eye of a hurricane, still and empty while her family and house-work whirled around her.

We had a cup of coffee and tried to pretend we could still be friends. But it was over. Our lives were going in completely different directions. I was shocked that she bored me, felt guilty because I wanted to leave. When I left, loneliness set in because I realized I had lost a friend. Later, I understood why I was so anxious to leave that kitchen. I was glad the drudgery and resignation she seemed to be facing had happened to her not to me. I thought of Doris Lessing writing about "lonely women going mad quietly by themselves, in spite of husband and children or rather because of them. . ." We were once friends—real friends—but times changed; we had changed.

Most of my future female friends would have lives more like mine—divorced or single, with careers, passing thirty and childless, having affairs of varying intensity, well-traveled, interested, optimistic, and curious. We really wouldn't trade in our lives for a mop and broom. But we, too, paid a price. Some of us wondered—as we fell asleep alone in a double bed, reading a book for company—whether we were any better off than our married, child-birthing sisters, and whether we would ever be able to have the best of both worlds.

One of the assumptions we live with is that we will always be supported by this network, this lifeline, of friends. A rift in a friendship can sometimes be repaired, but the actual physical death of a close friend (which has happened to some of us, particularly during the years of COVID) leaves a terrible void that cannot be filled.

We confirm ourselves through others, invest ourselves in others, use up and receive energy with others, measure our existence in relation to others with whom we share memory and history, and when the other person dies, a piece of us disappears with them. It is like another death. ". . . any man's death diminishes me, because I am involved in mankind, and therefore never send to know for whom the bell tolls; it tolls for thee," John Donne wrote.

When friends die, they take with them the words we shared, the emotions we felt, the vibrations of our special relationship. They take part of our history: They are no longer a living memorial and testament to ourselves.

Until the day when age hits us hard, most of us live as if we may just possibly escape death. We use euphemisms for death like "passed away" or "lost." Families and hospitals keep the terminally ill alive even when we know the person wants to die. We do all we can to forestall that final loss. After our our brains have shut down and our hearts stop beating and our lungs stop pumping, we get wired up and plugged in to keep from being declared dead. One of the great appeals of religion is its promise of an afterlife where we will once again reunite with our loved ones, and although I am a person of faith, my mind resists it as nothing more than metaphor.

Octavio Paz says that everything in the modern world functions as if death does not exist. "It is suppressed everywhere: in political pronouncements, commercial advertising, public morality and popular customs: in the promise of cut-rate health and happiness offered to all of us . . . the word death burns the lips." But our flight from death, the final isolation from this world, is a futile exercise.

In death, as in other forms of loneliness, the more we fear it and its implications the more we allow it to run our lives. The fear of death ironically makes some people self-destructive. They flirt with it and confront it again and again to prove they are not afraid.

A Zen Buddhist once told me he doesn't mourn the death of friends because he feels it is selfish. "You don't cry for the person's dying, but for yourself: You have lost something," he said. "If your favorite glass breaks, you look at the pieces and say: 'Oh no, not my favorite glass!' It's part of the same emotion you feel about death. You aren't concerned with the other person's dying; you are weeping over your own loss."

But most people cannot be so philosophical about it. They mourn, and mourning is a natural response to loss and essential to help us begin our lives again. When we suppress it, we have not really said goodbye to the dead, nor have we accepted the fact that our lives are fundamentally changed.

I learned of the death of a close friend while I was in Mexico. The accident that killed her was mentioned very briefly in a letter I received. I kept thinking the letter was a mistake. I was certain the wrong name was there, that whoever was dead must have had a name very similar to my friend's. It was a slip of the pen.

No one I was with had ever known her. No one could confirm her life, her aliveness. She might as well have been a dream.

I could not mourn. I felt isolated and trapped. Finally, I called her husband from one of the few town's few long-distance phones, located in a tortilla factory. He was accepting her death better than I was. Through him, I began to feel again and could think about her and begin the process of letting her go. But before that, when I could not sink into my sorrow and let it take me away, I was numb. I defaulted on my capacity to feel. This is what happens when we run away from our emotions. Unreality begins to pervade everything else we do and think, and the unreality cuts us off from everyone, like a high black wall between us and the living.

Funeral rituals sometimes help us face the hardest part of death: the physical disposal of the body—proof positive that the person we loved is really gone. Ceremonies give us a pattern to follow so we don't have to think. But this is not my way of mourning. Right now I want no rituals, for I feel like an actress playing a part. They are codified, unrelated in any way to the horror of a close personal loss. My own attempts at mourning are intemperate. I break and throw things. Sometimes I garden, for planting is an affirmation of life to me. I cannot be polite and social over tea or wine after someone I love has died. Yet I envy those who can and in so doing help one another through shared grief.

In whatever way healing works for us, we must get beyond mourning so we can live again. Some people stay immersed in it for years and are no longer open to the experience and risk of loving. People with terminal illnesses who know they are dying go through stages of denial, depression, and anger until they reach the final stage of peace and acceptance. To get to that last stage, the living must go through the same. There is no shortcut. People who can't mourn the death—of a loved one or a relationship—people who can't walk through loss and loneliness—live on with things left unresolved. Clinging to a person's memory to the extent of cutting us off from others has more to do with our own fear of loneliness and loss than with how deeply we loved someone.

I know a man and woman who were the best of friends. Eventually, they married. He had always been self-reliant, tough, cynical. She showed him that people aren't so bad after all. "My hard edges softened up," he said. "I began giving, smiling, reaching out. She made me see that if I opened up a bit I would find alternatives to being alone."

He in turn encouraged her to stay independent. He told her that if he made decisions for her, her identity would be diminished. She found she had a tremendous new vitality. Her self-assurance blossomed. "We're together not because we need to be," she told me, "but because we enjoy each other."

Three years after they were married, she was killed in a car accident on a snowy winter road. After her death, her husband said: "We didn't cling to each other in life, and I know she wouldn't want me to cling to her in death. She would want my life to go on. I would have wanted her to do the same."

This is what a good relationship is all about. If you need someone, then you are not free to love them. When you need someone, you have a vested interest in maintaining the dependency: If your lover or friend begins to grow away from you, you become threatened. When you can *choose* to love someone, when the need is gone, then there is no longer an irreconcilable conflict between commitment and freedom. As long as you are committed to be free—as long as you don't need to lean on someone else to give meaning to your life—then you can love freely. When you are strong enough to take the risks involved in loving, then you are able to accept the loss of love and go on living.

8

Living Alone

"Solitude is independence. It had been my wish and
with the years I had attained it. It was cold."
(Hermann Hesse, Steppenwolf)

The locksmith arrived to put a deadbolt lock on my front door.
As he got out his drill and bits, he asked me if I lived alone.
Yes, I lived alone, I told him. He began talking about the people
he meets in the city who live alone with multiple locks on their
doors and iron bars on their windows. Most of them live in fear.
Nearly half of the residents in New York City live alone.

"Why do you live alone?" he asked. I thought a minute and
answered: "Because I am more free, more independent." He tested
the new lock on the door, snapping the bolt up and down.

"You don't have freedom," he said. "All you have is convenience."

Yes, I thought later, *he is right*. I have privacy and mobility—I
can leave town tomorrow for Madison or Moscow. Yet sometimes
in the dead of night I wonder why I have chosen this solitary life.
I have in the past tried all kinds of other arrangements: I have
lived with a husband, with a lover, with roommates, in a cooper-
ative with two other people in which we each had our own bed/
sitting room and shared the kitchen. I have lived in a large country

house, a furnished room in Chicago, an apartment in France, near oceans and on mountains, with parents and brothers and pets and friends. But always I come back to this, to where I am now, among my locks and keys. I live alone.

The loneliness of living by yourself can be terrifying. I was reminded of this once when I was lying on a sunny rock and saw a small crab inches away, hurtling across the rock as if it were on fifty legs. *If we humans could run as fast for our size, we wouldn't need jets,* I thought. But when confronted with loneliness, it is as if I, too, sprout fifty legs and zoom the other way. That is how fast and frantic I am as I scurry from it, from the emptiness.

But when you live alone, where do you scurry to? I wondered. A few small rooms, a limited amount of carpet, wood, and tiles don't allow much running space. Sometimes I feel like the crab on the rock; I run for my life from the giant shadows that loom over me.

Sometimes this loneliness of my solitary life is comforting, and sometimes it is like a dull pain, and sometimes the loneliness is like hanging onto a cliff by the fingernails, and I claw and kick my way back to safety, using all my strength. The locksmith was right. This struggle is not freedom; it is not independence. It is solitary confinement. It is the torture of those condemned, as Sartre says, to be free.

It takes tremendous courage to choose to live alone, to let loneliness wash over you, overwhelm you, take up all your time, drain you, control you. It involves a battle with your greatest enemy—yourself—an exorcism in which you give loneliness all the footholds, all the advantages, before you begin to see the enemy and fight back. There are few front lines in the battle; it is more like guerrilla warfare.

There are as many reasons for living alone as there are people who do it. For some it is a permanent condition, but for most it is a way station. I have lived alone for three years. I do not know if in six months or a year or two I will feel the same need to be by myself, have my own space. But I have that need now.

Some psychiatrists and social workers say living alone can be harmful to your health, that it is an unnatural and unhealthy condition, that man is a social animal, and living alone is a break in the communal link.

"We're gregarious animals. People who are unable to connect, to live with other people, are hurt or injured in some way—by life experience, mothering, fathering—like the stereotyped old prospector who likes to be off by himself, wants no one to come near him. I don't consider that a natural condition," one psychologist told me. Philip Slater scorns living alone as "the psychic equivalent of holding your breath."

Because of our taboos on being alone, many people are programmed to feel lonely when they are by themselves, and stop feeling lonely when they are with other people.

"I can't stand to live alone," a magazine editor told me. "I need someone to reflect off; it is the only way I can assure myself I exist, that I'm not an illusion. It's like the tree falling in the forest. If no one hears it fall, then does it make any noise as it falls? If no one hears or sees me living, then am I really alive?"

Others argue living alone can be healthy, fulfilling, rewarding, soothing, that under certain circumstances, living alone can give people a real sense of autonomy, can bolster a sense of one's ego and self-sufficiency, can help people grow. "Sometimes being with others was so abusive and so overwhelming that it is a relief for people to be by themselves, to feel they don't have this overpowering figure burrowing into their unconscious, trying to find out everything that they feel and think," says therapist Leah Schaefer.

Another therapist I interviewed said that the best preparation for living with somebody is to first live alone. "If you learn to live with yourself, then you have less expectation that other people are going to provide answers for you. You won't think things like 'a baby will make things better' or 'I'll marry him and then he'll stop drinking.' Living alone teaches you how intricate life is. It requires additional skills. It is actually more complicated than living with someone because it involves a whole new set of ways of dealing with people, of judging each situation as unique, of learning who is responsible for what."

Sometimes I lean toward one view and sometimes toward the other, pretty much depending on which side I get out of bed in the morning. Sometimes I feel I am damned if I do and damned if I don't. I am seldom quite comfortable living alone unless I know someone is coming to visit, or I am going out that night, or away for the weekend. Yet I know I often feel better about myself, and less lonely, living by myself than I have in the past when I lived with people I could not connect to.

Why do people choose to live alone? A policeman told me his hours were too unpredictable and his work too dangerous to allow anyone else into his life. "Basically, I'm a loner," he said. "I take chances in my work. I'm tough and I plan to stay that way. I follow the rule of thumb: If any criminal gets close enough to kick me in the balls, shoot 'em. I don't want to pause in the middle of a risky job and say: 'What about Martha and the kids. . . ?' That hesitation is a sure way to die."

An anthropologist who lives alone told me: "I've never lived comfortably with an 'us' in my life; I am too egotistical for 'us.'"

A man who spent his childhood in hospitals says he has to live alone even though there is much about it he can't stand. "My discomfort with myself is a very essential problem," he says. "When I live alone I don't have to reveal the person I fear I am. I can't cope with people, with what is on the other side of the closed door of my house. It's like all the closed doors I grew up behind. Of course, I couldn't cope with what was in that room either—and what was in that room was me."

I know others, so many more, and each person has a reason, more or less credible, more or less healthy, for wanting to stay alone. I know two former nuns. Each has chosen a very different way of life. One wants to marry. The other, a beautiful woman with auburn hair and gold rings on her fingers, lives alone in a suburban apartment complex. She told me: "People expect me to marry. But I'm very happy living alone, and I'm willing to pay the social price. I have put a lot of work into learning about myself, coming closer to the center of my own being, unfolding the mystery of myself. The convent gave me the security I needed at the time. I don't need that kind of security anymore, even from a man. I have it in myself."

A social worker told me her life alone is the result of her parents' bad marriage. "I'm an only child and had to bear the brunt of the whole marriage," she said. "When my parents were around, I felt as if my own personality disappeared. I find to this day when I live with someone else, whether it's a lover or a roommate, that I pay too much attention to what that other person is doing or how he's reacting to what I'm doing, or how I appear in his eyes. When I'm by myself I can sit in my chair and listen to Bach and pick my nose and know I'm not reflecting off anyone else."

I ask myself: are these good reasons? Are they valid reasons? And should people who want to live alone have to give any reasons at all for their choice? It seems we must give reasons. We will struggle to assert our independence as long as we are unsure that independence is what we really want.

Psychoanalyst Karen Horney once told a reporter that "we move in three different directions in our relations: toward others, trusting and open; against others, healthy self-assertion; away from others, satisfying the need for occasional solitude. The person who feels a true sense of inner worth uses all three of these modes spontaneously, depending upon the realistic requirements of the situation."

We always balance the three against one another, and I suspect that people who live alone find they need more healthy self-assertion and solitude and fewer trusting, close relationships—at least for a while. Proximity and closeness can often be a threat. Without even a conscious awareness on our part, our instincts for self-preservation can make us arch and hiss like a frightened cat.

Many wild animals band together to survive. They move in packs and herds, often with the females and young in the center, and the strong males on the outside ready to protect against attack. There is a sense of interconnection, a unified purpose, one for all and all for one. We humans still band together—in hotels, office buildings, and in cities, for example. But the reasons and the effects are quite different from those of the jungles and the plains. As individuals, we do not band together for the purpose of common survival. Our purposes are at odds—even in the face of the threat of large death tolls posed by the COVID pandemic.

Usually, we are like swimmers swimming madly in parallel, roped-off lanes instead of people sharing a large pool. We can no longer identify the enemy. We fight each other for promotions, space, attention, money, and much else. In the situation we have created and perpetuate, retreating into isolation might be the surest way to survive. It protects nerves, stomach, and heart; it reduces wear and tear, prolongs life.

And there is another thing. To survive emotionally, we have erected barbed-wire defenses around ourselves so that in reaching out to other people, we often tear ourselves apart in the process, leaving little pieces of our psyche strung along a destructive fence of old regrets and past mistakes. Sometimes it is very painful to live with others, and sometimes we decide the pain just isn't worth it.

Living Alone

It is common for people who have been disillusioned by love to go through a period of isolation, of self-help therapy, getting their heads back together. This entire process often includes separation, living segregated emotionally and physically. This is a reason why some people I know live alone. They have gone through the terrible loneliness when the marriage or love affair begins to fade, the horror of thinking: "If I feel so lonely now with this person who I love, or once loved, how will I be able to bear it when I am alone?"

People often fail to recognize that the very presence of the other person makes them sense their loneliness and that when they are alone the loneliness actually goes away. The loneliness in marriage often comes from feeling trapped, knowing this empty day will be followed by a string of empty days, seeing no possibility for change or hope. If you are alone, at least the possibility of variety is there, the chance that tomorrow might be different, might present a new situation or person who can assuage the loneliness.

This period of isolation is often a time for reevaluation, healing old wounds, and for confronting your basic aloneness for the first time. Living alone gives the person who feels hurt and confused a chance to draw on untouched resources, to develop a new awareness of Self as an isolated and solitary individual, to confront what they have ignored or run from for years—perhaps for a lifetime. It is a time to learn that to love and be open to life may sometimes result in loneliness and that through pain, the heart learns to understand joy. A self-imposed aloneness gives some people a new sense of immediacy, a new depth, a new experience of total surrender to and reliance on one's self.

"Loneliness in marriage was a constant for me," a male friend told me. "The end of my marriage was a release. While I was with my wife, my loneliness was an implosion—an explosion that goes

111

inward. I became lethargic—sexually, professionally, every way. I had a continually deteriorating view of myself. My loneliness was like a bubble that has nothing inside, that is lighter than air, banging around inside a larger sphere. Finally she left me; her leaving saved me. The end was a reversal, an explosion outward. Of course, I was lonely then, too, but it was manageable. I handled it by assigning myself tasks: the task of losing weight, of reading. I changed jobs. I had an affair that made my sexual confidence soar. Now I live with a woman four days a week and by myself three days. I know I need time to be alone, and now I give it to myself."

For a while after my own first marriage, during the recuperation phase, I was a sexual separatist, living not only alone but apart from all social contact with men. I gave a small party during this time, and the women who came formed a tight circle in front of my fireplace. They kept their backs turned to the few men they brought along, who stayed like outcasts near my living room window. For some of the men, and for me, it was the first exposure to female chauvinism in action. I felt uncomfortable, yes, but I understood and even liked it. For relationships with men had drained me. I was battle-weary and gun-shy. I wanted nothing to do with men, needed time by myself to figure out my mistakes. I wanted a resting period, a sexual purge. I was tired of putting my ego on the line.

For a while, I didn't socialize at all. I lived in a furnished room and read *The Complete Sherlock Holmes*. I had maid service once a week, so for the first time, I didn't have to clean up after myself.

Then I met a woman who felt as I did, but who had gone a step further and committed herself to a life free of men. She did not socialize with men or sleep with them, but she was not a lesbian either. She had no sex life and planned to keep it that way.

She and I talked about our broken ideals, our plans for change. We put aside our romanticism and our masochistic behavior. We seldom talked about men. We talked about our weaknesses only to understand our strengths, the past only to build the future.

Then I met another woman who chose to socialize only with women, and then another until I realized that a lot of women had become sexual separatists. "There is a wonderful humanity, a great joy, in women being together at last," said one friend. "The less I see of men, the better I feel. I feel a tremendous calm, a freedom I have never felt before. Men try to steal my body and mind. Men urge me to be weak, while women urge me to be strong."

Many of the women I met during this time had been through psychotherapy, marriage counseling, and either a husband or disastrous love affair. Most of us, we learned, had first found a man and then found ourselves, and the two had been incompatible. As we began to grow, we felt that our growth hurt or threatened the men who had loved us as we were when we first met. We decided, each by our own route, to live free of men so we could work without guilt on our own potential.

We felt as Sylvia Plath writes: "The last thing I wanted was infinite security and to be the place an arrow shoots off from. I wanted change and excitement and to shoot off in all directions myself, like the colored arrows from a Fourth of July rocket."

Most of those women, including me, were not lesbian or bisexual as far as I knew—this was before open acceptance of sex and gender variations. All of us missed having sex with men. In some cases, abstinence was almost a spiritual purification. Male sexuality in its broadest sense had everything and nothing to do with our decision: It was the magnet that drew us together, yet, once together, we removed it from our immediate realm of concern. Men were not the issue; womanhood was the issue.

"I know I am a chauvinist, but I can't help but believe women are superior," said one twenty-four-year-old who hadn't socialized with men in three years. "My boss says I make him feel guilty for being a man. But I no longer attach any importance to what men say. They take up too much emotional space, don't leave me room to be myself.

"Women were brought up to empathize—perhaps too much so, for we often end up living in other people's shoes. But if I'm going to make a gift of my sensitivity to someone, they should be able to return it, so it is a circle we are both nourished by. Women can usually do that and men can't."

For most of us, a male-free life was a transition. We found out that those old Doris Day and Rock Hudson movies of our parents' and grandparents' day weren't telling the truth about love and happiness—that the truth was closer to Marlon Brando's kind of sex in *Last Tango,* where a man has superiority over a woman who finds pleasure in being degraded.

I have heard the term "man-hating" used to describe the feelings of women who go through this time of sexual separatism. Man-hating is, as defined by Ingrid Bengis in *Combat in the Erogenous Zone:* "A defense, a refusal, and an affirmation. It is a defense against fear, against pain. It is a refusal to suppress the evidence of one's own experience. It is an affirmation of the cathartic effects of justifiable anger."

Man-hating is an unfortunate term, perhaps coined by men who see the communion of mutually supportive women as a threat to their power. The phrase is too simple and negative to describe a phenomenon I found to be positive and constructive. Separatism among the women (and men) I knew then was more often an experiment in self-loving, in lifestyles, in focusing power within.

It was the first time in my life I identified with women, because I had always longed for my own sphere of power, and the power was in men. I was the man behind the glossy desk, the guy with the gun, never the woman waiting by the phone. (This was in my daydreams. In reality, I waited by the phone a lot.) I always felt compelled to ski, play tennis, and swim as well as my brothers, and if I didn't succeed, I always managed to tell myself I could if I tried harder.

Men had interesting jobs, money, and freedom, I thought. Women at that time got married, quit work, had babies, and lived in suburbs. I only reached the first step—marriage—and backed away. I was left with no one to identify with, trapped in my personal sphere of loneliness.

But the iteration of the women's movement that had begun by the 1970s changed that. Women began telling other women what they could become, even if it was at the expense of men who wanted us to stay as we were. Caught up in this rising wave of expectations, women left their husbands and lovers behind, and then were faced with the new loneliness of trying to communicate with only half the population—the female half.

Many of these women lived uneasily and in pain. "I tore my heart out for my husband," one woman recalled. "I was raised to feel if a man fucked me over it was okay, and if I loved him enough it would work out. Now it's changed for me. A man can't fuck me over and expect me to love him. Why in hell should I? I used up too much energy and anger, too many tears. Everything I believed in was torn down and battered. It took me a long while to rebuild my forces." This was said by a twenty-eight-year-old woman who went through a long period of celibacy before dating again.

Many of the women I knew then, while grateful for this new option, were at the same time uneasy with the position of female chauvinist. Any cause gone to the extreme can produce paranoia, blind hatred, and fear. But in its most constructive form, separatism was a positive force, a meditative retreat into ourselves in the company of other women who provided positive feedback. It was part of our growing pains, teaching us what we should have learned much earlier—how we must love ourselves before we can love others.

But of course, I paid the price for that little excursion into separatism. After a year of it, I went into group therapy to find out why I couldn't, or wouldn't, treat men as equals. An interesting scenario unfolded among the people I met in this group. From the beginning, I was sexually attracted to one of the men. Consequently, he was the only man I responded to or listened to. He was the only man who had anything important to say to me. He was also the only one I did not trust. This was an old syndrome: Because I liked him, I felt vulnerable before him. I sensed that I was giving him the power to hurt me, to reject me, to put me down.

The other men in the group noticed this and were understandably upset. They sensed how easily I dismissed them. I trusted them, yes, because they didn't threaten me. But I also didn't listen to them. I paid only surface attention; I was courteous but bored since there was nothing in it for me.

They did not let me get away with it; they howled in protest. At first, I denied it, then I cried, and when that had no effect on them, I dried my eyes. Gradually I began to see them as human first and male second, to see that they were as sensitive and pained as women, as confused and as lonely. A small thing, you might say—a basic, simple exercise in human understanding. I am not proud that it took me so long to break this pattern and end my role as a woman in constant battle with men. But I am proud that I broke it, for there are many women who never try and other women who don't try hard enough, and so never succeed.

There is, of course, another group of people who live alone, sometimes, but not always, by choice. In our society, which is structured like Noah's Ark, never-married singles can be made to feel like leftovers, residue, and the loneliness they feel is often a hollow emptiness. While much else has changed, never-married people—whether by choice or serendipity—are still often stereotyped: aunts cluck over unmarried nieces; mothers frown about unmarried sons; friends try to match-make. I have heard singles say they wish they could be married just once, to get the pressure off.

I have lived as a single woman in small towns, suburbs, and cities, and life around me always seemed to move two-by-two; people who were not paired up often felt out of place. Once-marrieds like myself felt the loneliness of trying to fill a gap left after life constructed around a partner crumbled. Never-marrieds often have a more frantic kind of loneliness—the kind that leads people to cruise online and in singles bars hoping to find the "right" person to fill the hole in their soul.

I used to go to singles bars in Chicago—places like the Original Mother's, Butch McGuire's, and O'Leary's. On the best nights, no one could move or hear. The jukebox roared, people jostled and sloshed drinks and laughed, and most of all, they looked. The bars seemed to be an undulating sea of eyes, blue, brown, black, gray eyes that nailed you to the wall with question marks. You? Are you interested? Interesting? Are you the One?

You didn't have to listen to people—often you couldn't hear anyway—all you had to do was watch the eyes. Vocal cords didn't count half as much as lips, teeth, weight, height, muscle tone, and stance. We were like horses pawing at the starting gate. I couldn't walk into the atmosphere without getting caught up in it. The messages were silent, but they were strong. We were looking for love.

Some years later in New York, I remembered those silent messages when I was walking down Seventh Avenue one night. I saw two men pass by each other, each apparently intent on his destination. In fact, each was checking out the other. Without turning heads, without pausing, each noticed on which side the keys hung from the other's belt and sensed the other's receptivity. I could almost feel their invisible antennae in the night. They passed one another, walked to their respective ends of the block, then turned around, nodded, and met again in the middle of the street, strangers no more and looking for love and the flush of warmth that sex can bring.

Until 1986, Grossinger's was a popular resort in the Catskills known for its singles weekend. The resort brochures warned that "many a girl returns home with nothing on the hook. But others make a lasting connection. . . ."

When I gave it a try, people I met were nice, shy, awkward, some attractive to me, some not, most trapped in dull jobs, and all went there for the weekend with celluloid smiles and mix-and-match jersey outfits. Over piles of kosher food one evening, a stunning redhead told me that she would marry any man who was good to her. She had lived five years with a businessman, she said. For the first four years, she had been indifferent toward him, and he doted on her. During the fifth year, she began to respond to his affection, and he immediately lost interest and moved out.

"Then I found out he was a sexual pervert," she sighed over her blueberry torte. "I didn't lose him to a woman. No, I lost him to Harry and Linda and Bob. . ." She ended up with a man "on the hook" that weekend. But the woman I shared my room with was not so lucky, nor was I. In the evenings, my roommate sat in the lobby wearing a modest black dress. It was her third singles weekend, and she was still looking, and I think of her more than I should these days, waiting with hands in her lap, a crumpled smile on her face. Just waiting.

No one I met there was looking for a quick lay, though some might have settled for that. They wanted someone to care about, and some were undoubtedly willing to act it out in bed first and talk about it later. There was a little bit of me in them, a bit of each of us who have ever felt lonely, felt a need to love one man, one woman. I went on Friday night ready to scorn, but when I left on Sunday I realized that we scorn most easily that which threatens us most. We are always lonely and always vulnerable to love: No matter how bitter and battered we may feel today, we will welcome the divine spark of love tomorrow, even though our longing is shot through with trepidation.

There is a church for singles in New York that my neighbor Lily P. forced herself to go to. Although she was uptight about it, she had given up on online dating, and a church seemed less threatening than a bar. After months of hesitation, she decided to take the chance. She dieted. She had her hair done. She dressed carefully and went.

"It wasn't bad," she concluded when I ran into her on our block after a few weeks. "Some of the people were decidedly unattractive, but some were good-looking. So I went back. Every time I went, I always found a person I was attracted to, and I would leave with him. I slept with some of them; I got hurt by some of them. At least they made me feel alive again, they set my emotions on edge.

"It's better than eating, which is what I usually do when I'm alone too long," she went on. "I made friends there. Some of the friendships were just time killers, true. But they filled a need. If you're hungry you sometimes have to go to McDonald's because it's the only thing around, even though what you really want is a filet mignon."

She is a pretty woman who talks fast and animatedly and struggles to keep her weight down. "I keep looking," she says. "I suppose I'm really looking for someone to mother me, take care of me, be close to me, hold me. But I'm afraid of being overwhelmed, of losing myself in someone else. I'm scared of the energy and anxiety, the neediness that drives me into relationships. I need someone to complete me, to give me a sense of my own worth. The problem is, as soon as I meet a man I am sexually attracted to, I don't feel good about myself. I feel I am being taken over, he has control over me. Of course, men aren't terrible people at all. But in my head I turn them into villains; I get hurt and I try to OD on chocolates."

When I was single and between marriages, I feared that I would forget how to compromise, how to share. I liked having someone in bed with me in the morning when I woke up. But a man got in the way of my morning rituals—the bathroom must be shared, the coffee made a certain way. I became afraid I would become so settled, my life so well-ordered, that there would no longer be room for one more.

The danger with living alone is that we become selfish. We forget how to give and give in on a day-to-day basis. A Catholic priest who lives alone and travels a lot told me he feared that as a result he had become "a very selfish person."

The selfishness, he said, comes because "I have only myself to care for and think about. I feel the need sometimes for the tenderness, the comfort of a close, real relationship. When I give retreats and everybody's paired up and I'm alone—that's when I feel loneliest. I'm getting on in age and slowing down, and now I feel that need for domestic rounding, a nest, roots. But I'm afraid it's too late to learn to share."

His work as a priest relieves the loneliness, he says, "but there are moments when I want to be loved close up. I need it, and I don't know what to do about it. I am determined to remain a priest, but against that, I feel the hunger and the rawness of my human needs. And, still, I've lived so long alone, I don't know how much ability I have left to really share."

Another man I know also feels that living alone is unnatural and selfish, but he can't imagine living with anyone since his divorce. He has lived alone for three years and he, too, is afraid of intimacy. "I can be a glib friend, but I can't open myself up. I think I'm afraid of the personal commitment—yet I also miss it. I like cooking, cleaning, keeping house, but I dislike what my life alone means. It means that I'm afraid, and that disgusts me. I was walking along the street today and looked at myself in the store windows and I thought I looked like clay. I suppose that comes from feeling all alone in the biggest city in the country. I thought: I am articulate, attractive, and earn a good salary. Yet I live in this great iceberg of fear. I feel like I can't make it on the market, the human market. If I were a cretin, then it wouldn't be quite as painful. But as it is I feel cheated. So I see my ex-wife occasionally."

Once I lived alone for far too long and began to question my sanity. On the streets I saw people who were broken and alone, mouths moving, mumbling, laughing to themselves, and I realized that one day my own solitary monologues might spill over, even turn into dialogues, self divided against self. I'm still afraid my lips may someday begin to move as I speak in my secret world, rehearsing again and again complicated and secret patterns, asking again and again questions without answers.

Once, in the middle of the night, I awoke from a dream, thumbed through the pages of *The Stranger* by Albert Camus, looking for a half-remembered phrase: "I heard something that I hadn't heard for months." That was it, from my dream. "It was the sound of a voice; my own voice, there was no mistaking it. And I recognized it as the voice that for many a day of late had been sounding in my ears. So I knew that all the time I'd been talking to myself."

They were the words of the character Meursault, who lives alone and free in his prison cell. I too am free, and yet feel caged within myself. *What is freedom*, I wonder. What price must be paid?

On Loneliness

A close friend of mine left her husband and lived alone for several years. She was lonely. She dreamed distorted dreams. In one of them, she watched a group of prostitutes get ready to service the evening crew of a ship. One whore touched her clitoris softly, and it puffed out, ready. A voice in her dream whispered to her: "Touch it, and it weeps for you, it weeps for the world." My friend awoke from the dream with legs apart, moist, and she too wept. When she saw her husband again, she told him that she missed being touched. "That's the price you'll have to pay," he answered.

When she told me about it, she looked stunned. She said that, as she lived alone, she could feel fear slowly rise inside of her. She slept and drank too much. Her world of freedom threatened to drown her. She procrastinated. She sometimes ate until she vomited. For the first time in her life, she said, she did nothing to deny that she was growing old with a hole in her soul.

She did not laugh for weeks, not even once. Then for weeks her laughter was high, almost hysterical, and seemed to come only from the surface and did not penetrate her soul. She asked me if, once you have learned to be alone, you can ever really love again. "I feel like I have a core of scar tissue inside of me, and it keeps me numb," she said. She found herself doling out emotions in portions, like chocolate on ice cream. I could not help her; I had no answers.

At last, she bought a double bed. She told me her single bed confirmed her isolation, while the double bed at least acknowledged new possibilities. She met a man she wanted to have sex with, but she didn't let it go that far. Instead, she thought of the morning after, the parting, the emptying, and she was still afraid of her vulnerability. A vice tightened around her until she was deadlocked. "I have privacy, independence, my work. I should feel good. Instead, I feel alienated. I got what I wanted, and I'm not happy with it. My freedom is a burden and a chore."

Living Alone

She made new friends and finally had an affair. But those friends also lived alone, and it sometimes occurred to her that all they had in common was a quivering mass of neuroses and that they huddled together pudding-like for comfort. As for the love affair, it seemed almost impersonal, she said. She found herself bored and wished the man would not stay the night.

She and a psychiatrist who lived alone became lovers. She did not ask him about other women. She did not care and, consequently, she was not jealous. Other people could not break them up or bring them closer. It was, she thought ironically, a solid and unshakeable affair. She wondered if this were ideal love. Maybe the secret was not to care enough. It was pleasant and painless.

But gradually she became afraid of her lover. As she got to know him better, the rooms of his house seemed barren and dead, the walls had nothing to hold them together. He seemed restless and edgy. She suspected he had lived alone too long, and she feared her exposure to it. She felt guilty about leaving him, and wondered after she left she why she persisted in carrying that small messy baggage of guilt with her wherever she went.

Bertrand Russell wrote: "Many people, when they fall in love, look for a little haven of refuge from the world, where they can be sure of being admired when they are not admirable, and praised when they are not praiseworthy. To many men, home is a refuge from the truth . . ."

In my marriage, my home had been a refuge from the storm inside myself. When I left, the storm was unleashed. I could not escape anymore, could not flee anywhere. One friend of mine left his wife and then ended up in a psychiatric hospital. Another who lived alone tried to kill himself. But I plodded on, mercilessly sane.

Eventually, I understood that you can't lie to yourself about loneliness. You just learn how to deal with it, or you fail to learn how to deal with it, just as you learn how to handle being too fat or thin, short or tall, or having a clubfoot. I doubt if I will ever again be as lonely as I was when I first realized how little I liked myself. When I am lonely now, it is usually part of the loneliness of ordinary living, and not the loneliness of self-doubt and despair, of not knowing who you are inside.

When I am lonely, I will reach out for anyone, call an acquaintance, plan dinners, go to movies—anything to fill time. Such loneliness and the frantic activity it generates can eventually lead to depression. When I am depressed, it does not occur to me to call my closest friend. I huddle in my shell and am surprised at my enormous relief when someone calls me. But I don't want to see them. I feel dragged down, unable to make decisions. Nothing I do brings joy. Such depression feeds our loneliness; we tend to impose our own isolations on ourselves. It is a circle: depression to loneliness and back again to depression.

The danger of living alone is that there is no one else around to challenge your moods, to question you, to draw you out. You must sit yourself down and give yourself a talking to: ask yourself—why do I feel bad? If you can pinpoint what is making you feel bad, then you can handle it more easily. Ask yourself: Do I have enough friends? Do I have friends who don't fill my needs? Is my work bothering me? Am I angry with my lover? What is keeping me away from meaningful contact with people? Then you must decide on the best path out of the maze. But before you decide on any course of action, you must first be sure you have been honest with yourself and that you are not once again maneuvering just to avoid confronting the reality of your loneliness.

I have learned it is most important when when living alone to remember to be good to yourself. Eat at the table from a plate and not on the couch from a paper container. Buy fresh vegetables even though you can't finish them all. Get yourself a present on your birthday. Tell yourself you deserve it; chances are you do.

Make your house or apartment comfortable and pleasant to look at, so you look forward to coming home. Hang some pictures on the walls, buy a bright rug and fresh flowers. It is a luxury to live alone. Many people try but cannot make it, cannot afford it, either financially or mentally. Living alone makes you see that the great irony of loneliness is that it has nothing to do with how other people feel about you, but how you feel about yourself.

9

Emotional Anesthesia

"Because he'd given up, the surface of life was comfortable
for him. He worked reasonably hard, was easy to get along with
and, except for an occasional glimpse of inner emptiness . . .
his days passed quite usually."

(Robert Pirsig, Zen and the Art of Motorcycle Maintenance)

I was walking one winter day with a friend through a park in Illinois. We were talking quietly when suddenly we heard the howling of a dog. The dog sounded in great pain. We followed the sounds and found a man beating a golden retriever puppy with a stick. His wife and two children looked on, powerless and silent. The puppy didn't move, and the more the man hit it, the more it cringed. As we came closer, we could see the puppy's front legs were so wobbly with fright that it couldn't stand up.

We watched for a moment from a distance, shocked. Then my friend broke into a run across the grass, screaming at the man to stop. But he kept hitting the weak and whimpering puppy, even as she stood there shouting at him. He was a large man and paid no attention whatsoever to her. I watched, hesitated a moment, and then I, too, ran over to the man—more to rescue my friend than the dog. With the two of us there, he put down the stick. His wife lifted the trembling puppy in her arms, and the family walked away.

I was numb. I told myself the beating was none of my business. There was nothing I could do about it. What right had I to interfere? My friend, however, was shaking with rage. I tried to calm her. I told her she was overreacting, that it is a fact of life that animals are mistreated, that the injustice of it is small compared to child abuse. I was reasonable and righteous, and she would not be reconciled.

It sickened me to lecture her, but I could not stop. It horrified me to realize I could watch a dog being beaten and hesitate before trying to do something about it. Later, I would have nightmares about it. I knew that a passing child would have screamed and cried for that dog, that any healthy, spontaneous adult would have at some point reacted as my friend did. What had happened to me? Why was I numb, anesthetized, and dulled into silence?

"If life is beating dogs and brutality," my friend cried that winter day, "then how do I learn to handle life as it is?" I could not answer. I felt an emptiness inside. I wanted to reach out and comfort her, but something stopped me.

When I see abuse or cruelty on the street, it's as if I run my responses through a computer chip that launches the controls to execute indifference. I watch and weigh and wait. They say the safe thing is to walk away and people who can do this are to be admired for not losing their cool. But where do we draw the line?

I believe we *don't* react because we *can't* react. It's no longer safe to react. If we responded to the cruelties we see in real life or online, we wouldn't be able to bear it; we would be screaming in the streets. To protect our sanity, we refuse to react and become automatons. We bury our feelings deep inside. We become unable to relate to what people do and who they are. This icy internal silence is hard on me. I am a fragmented person in a nation of fragmented people.

When did we all start feeling this way? Was it 9/11? Mass shootings of children in schools, of people at worship? The murder of John F. Kennedy? Dr. Martin Luther King Jr.? Watergate? Attica? Kent State? Bloody body bags from endless wars? Race-hate murders on our streets? All became part of our emotional geography. Assassinations and bombings part of our common fare. We reacted first with outrage and then with silence, our attention distracted by new cruelties.

"When death is everywhere and on such a vast scale it becomes indifferent, impersonal, inevitable, and finally, without meaning" says Alvarez. "The only way to survive . . . is by shutting oneself off utterly from every feeling, so that one becomes invulnerable, not like an armored animal but like a stone."

Long after Kennedy's assassination, he remained a symbol of a time when we could believe, things made sense, and it all would work out for the best. In our inherited DNA, we still feel the grief for that lost innocence and trust. It makes no difference that history tarnished the Kennedy myth or that he was as compromised, trapped, and flawed as any other man. The point is, he was seen as our personal president.

He was the last public figure to be our father, our lover, our brother, our son. In documentaries and old news clips we see Jackie Kennedy's dress covered with blood, hear how she refused to change it because she wanted to "let them see what they have done." We never asked who "they" might be; I have a sickening feeling now that she may have meant all of us.

Since then, each generation has been exposed to increasing random violence through the internet, social media, gaming, crime shows, newscasts, disinformation, and daily life. We see images of slaughtered children, starving babies, war-torn body parts. We read about weapons sold for profit to any buyer, the violence of the ever-growing gap between rich and poor, the daily destruction of our environment; we see despair and addictions ruining the lives of those we love—and know we can do nothing about any of it.

It was in the 1960s that the movie industry produced *The Graduate,* which is about a young man's alienation from the hypocrisy he saw in society. Dustin Hoffman, who played the main character, alternated between withdrawing into silence and shouting in frustration as he tried to fit into a society he could no longer relate to. In the 1970s, this same disintegration and rage boiled over into violent films like *Death Wish* and *Taxi Driver,* in which quiet men slaughter strangers out of desperation and random murder is the only relief valve left—the final catharsis.

Twenty years ago, many of us would have been outraged and astonished by movies with heroes who are assassins and mass murderers . . . by popular TV shows filled with gratuitous violence. Now, we are silent when we see them. Some of us even empathize. We all understand that it has happened in real life. People have become numbed by what they see around them and have lost a traditional sense of morality. We don't know how to handle it anymore.

The result is that we create new laws to regulate violence but that end up punishing the poor, protecting the rich, and creating more problems than they solve. We saturate ourselves with rules until, it has been estimated, average American citizens are now governed by almost eight million laws. With more regulations, we become more anesthetized.

An article in *Harper's Magazine* more than a decade ago noted that "The majority of Americans have become like children surrounded by too many noes—withdrawn, passive, apathetic." We do not know whom to blame or where to relieve our frustration. There is nothing left but vast indifference.

I know a man in his eighties who lives surrounded by things from the forties: an RCA turntable, seventy-eight-rpm records, suits with wide lapels, a bulky floor-model television with fading tubes. I asked him why he clings to the past and he responded, "Because that was the happiest time of my life. Things made sense to me then."

Nothing seems to make sense anymore. We have only to step outside our door to realize how we no longer respond to the incongruous. It costs more to buy organic, unprocessed foods than foods that have been doctored with colors and chemicals. We spend large sums of money on gadgets we seldom use; some of us throw away clothes after one or two seasons. Each of us, on average, throws out more than one hundred pounds of food a year.

A few years ago, I watched some Americans in Paris taking pictures of one another in front of Notre Dame. They took the time to carefully set up and shoot the photos, but they raced through the cathedral they came to see. The picture is what they were after—the surface of the substance. In public places we often hear Muzak instead of Mozart, as if we are being deliberately numbed—pacified with insipid material for mass consumption. This year I suffered through twelve hours of Muzak at the DMV waiting to get my driver's license renewed and later learned that the man who invented Muzak said, "It is to hear and not to listen to."

I assume as a matter of course that advertisers, politicians, and businessmen lie. I hear that an automobile manufacturer advertised the clarity of its car windows by rolling them down before the commercial was filmed, that a major soup company put marbles in the bottom of a bowl of soup to push the vegetables to the top for an ad. Useful and reliable products that once lasted a lifetime now come designed to fail within a few years.

I am mildly surprised that none of this surprises me. I wonder when it will end and who will end it.

I went into a hardware store the other day to buy a mousetrap, knowing I might not actually walk out with one because it is a cruel way to kill a mouse. I expected to be told they were no longer made or to be confronted with a dozen options: two-mouse mousetraps; enclosed mousetraps; steel mousetraps; triangular, square, and round mousetraps. The salesman took me over to the mousetrap bin. I looked at the mousetraps before me. They were the same practical, effective, longlasting wooden and metal-spring mousetraps of my youth! I wanted to dance in the aisles, forgetting momentarily the cruelty. They really *didn't* build a better mousetrap! I could hardly believe it! This mousetrap in my hand was sane and understandable. It made sense to me. It was cheap and simple. It caught mice. That mousetrap made me feel on balance again, but also revealed to me how far I have descended into cynicism.

Where can we place the blame for these bleak changes in our lives? Many of us pounce on new technologies, and often we are justified. Computers and tablets and cellphones are in almost every home, office, and pocket because we choose to put them there. We lean on them because they are efficient, convenient, open us to the world, and speed things up.

They also create new anxieties, sometimes hourly. "Without my cell phone, I might as well be dead," the daughter of a friend told me. "It's frightening to live without being able to instantly push a button to talk to someone."

They have proven to be not only a powerful tool for connecting people but a wickedly effective platform for fomenting and organizing hate without consequences. They have led to—and highlighted—a disintegration of bonds that once held us together as a country.

But this phenomenon is nothing new to people of the Baby Boomer generation. Television was the first technology to bring the power of images into homes. Families enjoyed years of shootouts in *Gunsmoke* along with fake punches and deaths. They didn't respond negatively to this brutality when they saw it at the time, but they were getting their first lessons in buffering emotions.

Harry Guntrip did a groundbreaking study of a group of children who were shown a TV program in which boys and girls attacked another child their age. The young viewers were then taken into another room where the researchers had placed a child-sized doll. Without exception, each one ran to the doll and beat it up.

Children are great imitators. In the study, they couldn't separate their reality and instead imitated what they saw on television. We adults, however, are good at buffering—a process in the brain that reduces the impact of negative events. Since the advent of the internet, we seem to be buffering more and more to the point of numbness, accepting images of brutalities that would once have made us turn away.

This numbness toward the outside world can creep into our personal one as well. When my first marriage foundered and failed, I was so numb from a destructive job that I didn't trust my instincts when it came to my romantic partner. The therapist told me to share why I thought I should stay married. When I tried to list the reasons, I felt as if I were standing outside myself, watching—a disassociation that could happen in the devastation of any failed romance but in my case was extreme. My voice choked. I couldn't think of any reasons that seemed valid. I could hardly speak. Then he told me to give all the reasons why I should leave my husband. The tears stopped. I spoke calmly, firmly, and to the point. I felt good when the session was over. But I still did not trust my instincts.

Then the therapist played back on a tape all that I had said. I listened to myself for the first time in a long while. When I tried to give the reasons for staying, I sounded like a martyr and a whining child! When I gave my reasons for leaving, I sounded strong and compassionate, as if I knew how to take care of myself.

Why hadn't I been able to listen to myself before? Why did I value the words coming out of my mouth so little? When I tried to *act* on my own, I failed, but when I finally *reacted* to a machine that threw my voice and suffering back at me, I saw clearly.

I had been conditioned to respond to what I heard rather than trusting what I felt. All of us are vulnerable to some extent. Americans now spend more than seven hours a day watching videos, browsing social media, and "swiping our precious hours away" on tablets and smartphones. Add the screen time at our jobs, and most of our days are chewed up by inter-*net* rather than inter-*personal* interactions, making it easier for us to find fewer reasons to talk to one another.

These technologies can make us discount people around us and ourselves. We become viewers in every sense of the word, feelings buried.

"The more connected we become with our phones, computers, and virtual relationships, the less we look each other in the eye or have actual conversations. We represent ourselves on social media almost as a self-marketing strategy. This creates a new kind of loneliness, particularly for those viewing others' seemingly perfect lives while perhaps making comparisons to something not quite so perfect in their own lives," says Jane McLoughlin-Dobisz, guiding teacher at the Cambridge Zen Center in Massachusetts.

Robert Pirsig warned us in his 1974 book, *Zen and the Art of Motorcycle Maintenance*—long before the advent of the internet—that television, the first screen-based media in our homes, had already started to convince people that "what's around them is unimportant. And that's why they're lonely. You see it in their faces . . . first the little flicker of searching, and then when they look at you, you don't count. You're not what they're looking for."

Advertising preys on our insecurities and alienation and encourages us to find solace in things. "No one knows about loneliness better than Madison Avenue," said a friend who works in the business. We often buy things online or in stores to reassure ourselves of our uniqueness. A friend told me that almost every weekday afternoon she drives to the local mall. "I buy a bathtub mat, a coffee mug, some small thing. I don't have much money. But I buy things to feel I exist. To select one item from among an array of things makes me feel I have taste, I can choose, I have some control in my life, I am still an individual."

But whether we are scientists or poets, we have become like interchangeable cogs in a nonstop machine. We have become digits and codes, our given names seldom used as the main way to identify us. Everything we use and eat is rolled off an assembly line; our garbage looks similar from coast to coast. We fuel proliferation that is the physical and moral cancer of our time: an endless destruction of our environment matched by an endless reproduction of once-useful material that finally smothers and kills us.

As a country, we glut ourselves on a massive amount of mood-soothing drugs, both illegal and prescription, and on fat and sugar for the same reason that we glut our lives with objects: Because while we're doing it, we feel good. No matter that we feel guilty afterward when the reckoning haunts us. It gives us a fast fix. It tranquilizes us into feelings of peace with ourselves. A full belly and an anesthetized brain help us avoid our feelings of alienation and loneliness.

On Loneliness

I know a woman who is extremely overweight and is afraid to lose the excess pounds. When she is thin, she feels she does not exist. "I don't overeat when I feel happy or sad, just when I feel numb," she says. "I eat to fill the empty spaces."

All these things—the addictive food, fast cars, faster computers and constant pings of phones in our pockets and purses—serve as a bulwark against our pain, our sense of isolation and futility. I suspect that this is the real reason for their prevalence and importance in our lives. The problem is that these panaceas never work for long; we are wired to want more.

These electronic data systems that now infiltrate nearly every waking moment of our lives are concerned not with the creation of whole and healthy human beings but with tapping into our needs for instant self-gratification. We have allowed it, loved it, become digitized of our own free will. It drives the need for longer workdays in sometimes numbing jobs—a sacrifice we make in order to get money to feed the systems that feed our need to buy more things.

These systems by nature separate what we do from the essence of who we are and as a result fuel our loneliness, impotence, and anger. "There is no villain, no 'mean guy' who wants us to live meaningless lives, it's just that the structure, the system demands it," says Pirsig. I find myself wondering who puts the stitches in my sandals, who runs the machines that produce tampons and hot dogs. I wonder if they feel valuable, useful, integrated. We are lucky if we find jobs that coincide with what we want from life and how we want to be remembered when we die. But if we are among the unlucky ones, it is an experience that shatters and splinters us. Our visions become distorted bits and pieces, our images reflected in broken mirrors.

In our frustrations, we don't know where to turn and so we move around looking for a better life. We surge from coast to coast like water in a shallow sea, as if drawn helplessly by forces beyond our control. At some point, we must face the fact that there is nowhere left to run.

For a while, I was a notorious mover. A friend finally wrote to me in despair: "Have you ever considered a mobile home? Or, alternatively, can't you ever be satisfied?" I was restless in Wisconsin and Illinois, and finally, I ended up in New York. As an isolated Midwestern farm girl, the things I saw in the city astounded me.

The first day, I saw a man with no legs glide down the street on a skateboard. I saw a white man run out of a delicatessen with a machete in his hand, pursuing a Black man. I saw buildings of glass that reflected clouds. I had never before felt such warmth from people I just met or such hostility from strangers. I never saw such beauty or such pain in people's eyes. Unlike reticent Midwesterners, New Yorkers talked freely about their emotions—in shops, at restaurants, while waiting for a light to change. I was thrilled to hear people speak so openly of their feelings, even to strangers, thinking it might help me better understand my own. The city was like a piston, driving the country forward, and I was content. But the sense of not belonging, not believing, of meaningless events, followed me to the East Coast and tracked me down.

One of the first friends I made told me that she had heard the sound of gunshots in her apartment building. She did not call the police. "What good would it do?" she asked. "There are two hundred families in the building. Are the police going to search each one?" A few days later, the hallway began to smell. She thought a cat had died. The smell grew stronger. Finally, someone called the police. They broke down the door across the hall and found the body. The smell of death had soaked into the walls. The man who came to repaint the apartment left the door open and the radio on and whistled while he worked.

I couldn't believe that death could be treated so casually, so cynically. Yet, what choice do we have? When a plane carrying dozens of orphans from Vietnam crashed and burned, I became so distraught that I stopped reading the New York papers. Those who continued to listen to the news explained to me that I took it all too seriously, too personally. Yet, when I missed being blown to bits myself by a bomb planted in La Guardia Airport, I felt nothing. My own brush with death barely affected me. I took it casually because—just because there seemed no other way to take it.

This attitude crops up everywhere. I went into my beauty parlor on Bleecker Street and was struck again by the same lack of feeling. The hairdresser pointed to a woman on the cover of a fashion magazine.

"See her?" he said, clipping away at my ends.

"She's dead. She just killed herself. She did it with pills, left a note. She was twenty years old."

I felt the cold blade of the scissors along the back of my neck.

"She told a friend that her life's ambition was to be a cover girl. That's what happens when your dream comes true and you find out it's a bore," he said.

This numbness, this inability or unwillingness, to respond spills over into other areas of my personal life. Shortly after I moved to New York, the editor of a major magazine called me and said he wanted to talk about an assignment. I met him at his office, and he took me out for lunch. Before lunch, we ordered Bloody Marys. I told him about the articles I had in mind. He looked at my silk blouse and told me that I had lovely breasts. I kept on talking about my ideas, eager to get an assignment. After two hours, I said I was hungry, but by then the dining room was closed. After another Bloody Mary, he put me in a taxi and kissed me goodbye. I never heard from him again. I couldn't believe I had allowed myself to be treated so disrespectfully and cynically (this was before my feminist enlightenment). We had talked for almost four hours without him saying anything of significance regarding the assignment.

Emotional Anesthesia

We have many ways to communicate; a constellation of satellites bounces our voices back from outer space. Yet, too often we can't actually talk to each other. And there are no words for this emotional anesthesia I feel, only a dull, inarticulate pain shored up with a list of incidents like my afternoon with the editor. I can't, for some reason, integrate them. The grievances stay like an undigested lump in my belly. It doesn't help at all to lay blame on anyone or anything.

I think I am, by the life I lead, contributing to my debilitation. Instead of going to a small college, I went to a large university. Instead of working for a small business, I joined a large corporation. I closed myself inside a high-rise office. Then I went to work for myself and lived alone. I thought that if I weren't lost in a large group, then perhaps I would feel more like an individual. But individualism, as I practiced it, didn't work.

"There is nothing like the pursuit of individualism to make us feel disconnected, bored, lonely, unprotected, unnecessary, and unsafe," Philip Slater points out. I can eat take-out food and watch movies on my laptop. I can, if I want, go for days without really talking to anybody about anything significant—that is, anything that has to do with my survival. I am crowded into streets and public buildings with people I do not know, and so I feel insignificant.

The percentage of people who live by themselves increases every year. I would like to peel away the facades of those apartments-for-one the way I would strip a lid off a sardine can and peer inside to see how those other loners work and play, where they look for love, and whether they too feel frozen inside.

Dreamers of the American dream long ago went into hibernation. They speak of it with either nostalgia or scorn, but no hope of achieving it. Surveys show that most people no longer expect a materially better life next year; they are just trying to hold their own. I was a dreamer of the American dream, and I too have dropped out. I am helpless before our massive wealth inequality, race discrimination, failing educational and health care systems, corporate cabals that make essential prescription drugs unaffordable, lobbies for guns, coal, oil, toxic fertilizers. I know that my attitude perpetuates my helplessness.

As Slater says, every time we smile politely when the government or some corporation tramples on us, we encourage their inhumanity. Sometimes I think the symbol of America should be changed from the eagle to the vulture.

But I have not given up, which I find rather curious. Maybe this emotional anesthesia is a way of buying time. Maybe my numbness is like scar tissue that enables old wounds to heal.

Perhaps it is, for now, the best way I can handle this pervasive sense of being strangers in a strange land. The answers are cloudy, and all I am left with are these ruminations. I only know that if our discomfort makes some of us withdraw and be afraid, then perhaps when pushed far enough we will do something to end our alienation and cultural loneliness, do something to bind our wounds and integrate our lives again.

10

Soul Searching

"We shall not cease from exploration
And the end of all our exploring
will be to arrive where we started
and know the place for the first time."

(T. S. Eliot, "Little Gidding")

For many years, I looked for ways to rid myself of the habits that isolated me and made me lonely. In trying to discover, or rediscover, the real emotions beneath my social veneer, I journeyed through half a dozen therapies, movements, and faith-based organizations.

I was helped a little by each of them. By putting together bits and pieces of the insights they offer, I have uncovered some of the dynamics behind my loneliness. I found out how to use my loneliness creatively instead of letting it destroy me.

Early in this journey, I met many people who were activists in the 1960s but a decade or two later wondered why they had bothered to wear themselves out and why their dream for social change fell through. Some were sidetracked by drugs; some exhausted by battle fatigue. Relationships went sour. They began to doubt what they believed in.

On Loneliness

A former spokesman for the Vietnam Veterans Against the War told me: "After I was arrested for the eighty-fourth time, and spending more time in jail than out, and trying to get bail quickly enough so I could rush home and see myself on television, I finally realized what an ego trip I was on. I was screwing every woman in sight and then wondering why no relationship meant anything to me. I was part of an elitist group, and we thought we were speaking for America."

For many activist leaders, their struggle for social change gave way to a search for internal harmony and peace. As a psychiatrist noted at the time, "Belief in society and its ability to change enabled people to repress their personal unhappiness and to find purpose in their lives . . . But after the sixties, social distress and private unhappiness coincided; political and social movements now reflected and reinforced private disbelief and disaffection." Therapy and meditation groups, along with the weary radicals they attracted, appeared laughable, confusing, and hypocritical to many at the time, including me.

I had friends in Woodstock, NY, who I was visiting from time to time throughout the 1970s and 1980s. Two decades after the Woodstock Festival,* I still saw former protestors on the streets there, some strung out, some broke, some lolling in cafes, most of them stoned. I saw others sleeping at the bus stop in the town square, talking to themselves and looking lost.

Those who didn't stay embedded in the past moved on to self-help groups rooted primarily in non-Western philosophies: transcendental meditation, est (Erhard seminars training), yoga, encounter therapies, gurus, sanghas—each concerned with inner wholeness and eliminating alienation and loneliness. These

---

* More than 400,000 people attended the Woodstock Festival in 1969, named after the town of Woodstock, NY. The festival, however, was not held in Woodstock but on a local dairy farm after town residents opposed it.

philosophies presume that each person can become a self-confident, secure, warm, creative, joyful, and spontaneous human being and that this "real self" is blocked by the tensions created by our rearing and society.

They believe, as did humanist psychologist A.H. Maslow, that the ideal person "knows the world, its vices, poverties, quarrels, tears and yet is able to rise above them and to . . . see the beauty of the whole cosmos." Their goal is to feel at one with the universe rather than strangers to it, to have "a sense of belonging versus ostracism, isolation, aloneness, rejection."

Many former activists began to feel that significant social change comes from the inner harmony of each person rather than group pressure and mass protest. When publicity-hound Jerry Rubin announced that he wanted "to be left alone to find out who I am," he was simply reflecting what many of us learned from the turmoil of the 1960s: that our national inability to communicate—and our personal feelings of being duped, left out, and impotent—is made of up of millions of individual personal failures to communicate.*

My skepticism didn't last long. The burden of my frustration during the breakup of my marriage became so great that I finally realized I needed outside help. I could no longer manage or cope on my own. But I didn't know how to go about getting help. I didn't trust Western therapy or consciousness-raising groups. I was not a joiner in any sense.

As a matter of fact, during most of the sixties, I stayed at arm's length from marches and protests. I was maced during the Dow Chemical riots at the University of Wisconsin, but only because I was passing through. I was chased by Chicago police at the 1968 Democratic convention, but only because I was a journalist in

---

* A phenomenon that has grown worse and now threatens our very democracy.

the vicinity. I didn't go South for voter registration; I didn't go East to the White House. I didn't even know much about Reverend Martin Luther King Jr. until the day he was murdered. Perhaps this hesitancy and just plain ignorance were because I was scared: I was the first in my family to go to college, my road out of poverty, and my scholarships would be taken away if I were arrested. More likely I was wrapped up in my little white world full of indifference and didn't care. Or maybe I just didn't care enough to find out.

In any case, I remember sitting in France in 1967 defending the American right to be in Vietnam. That was how little I knew or cared. I never committed myself. I never joined. Temperamentally, I thought it would be easier for me to be a guerrilla revolutionary, working on my own, rather than to join a mass protest. Those grand injustices everyone was shouting about had little to do with my misery, alienation, or loneliness.

The women's movement of the 1970s planted the first seed of hope in my barren soul. When I read the first issue of *Ms.*, I was struck by the fact that so many other women had the same problems I had. Although I resisted being branded a feminist, I identified completely. I found companions, sisters, if only on paper; my loneliness eased.

With the women's movement I began to see for the first time that I could learn about myself and my marriage by sharing my experiences with other people. Their support made me strong enough to branch out and make one of the most important and specific decisions of my life: I began transcendental meditation (TM).

Meetings were held at the Palmer House in Chicago. I went as a reporter and stayed as a participant. I found after seven lessons that TM was not a religion but a source of inspiration, that it could help me clear up problems in my life and make me feel whole. I began to practice TM alone at home.

Each time I silently repeated the mantra that had been given to me—two syllables of ancient Sanskrit that are supposed to help your mind transcend thought to a state of pure consciousness—my mind seemed to enter a neutral state free of extraeonus thoughts. As I meditated, my facial muscles relaxed, my breathing slowed, I could feel my head nodding lower and lower. The muscles in my arms twitched involuntarily as if I were falling into a deep sleep. Yet I stayed alert, acutely conscious of the noises around me. It was an extremely pleasant sensation, almost as if I were watching myself take a nap.

Although science has now validated the value of meditation, I didn't believe at the time that TM could do much for me. I only believed in what I could see, feel, hear, and touch. But meditation changed all that.

One evening, something happened that prodded me into an unwilling belief about the benefits of meditation. I usually kept an alarm clock tucked between the couch cushions during meditation so I could peek at it to see when twenty minutes (the suggested duration for meditation) had passed. This evening, the alarm went off accidentally. The shock was immediate.

My eyes opened wide, my heart pounded frantically, my limbs were weak and shaky, my stomach was queasy. In short, I felt as if I had surfaced too fast from a deep dive. And my first question was: Where have I come back from? What is happening to my mind during these thoughtless, timeless minutes?

That night I acknowledged for the first time that I had changed since starting meditation three months earlier. I had more energy, drank less, and, most importantly, felt less trapped by my marriage and job. All the traps were still there, but they didn't seem to hurt as much. Now I was aware I could do something about them.

Sometimes I would look at my husband and realize how bad things were, and yet it didn't bother me as it had before. It was as if there were an invisible shield between him and me. I could see us interacting as before, but a part of me had stepped aside as a dispassionate observer. I had distance and perspective. I felt more centered in myself, more confident, less insecure—certainly less lonely.

We now know meditation does produce physiological changes that can reduce tension in the body, increase perception, and generally make life more enjoyable. But at the time, it was considered in the realm of quacks. Dr. Herbert Benson, the founder of the Mind/ Body Medical Institute at Harvard Medical School, was one of the first to study the effects of meditation on the brain and confirm that it is a therapy that lets us "control ourselves and our reaction to our stressful environments." It certainly did that for me.

I was working at a Chicago newspaper at this time, and twenty minutes of meditation in the afternoon kept me calm until quitting time. TM gave me the emotional distance to also see how bad my situation was at work, and I left the job. It kept me on an even keel. I found the confidence to seek freelance work.

Was it *all* due to TM? Probably not. The timing and a level of despair made me desperate. But TM certainly set me on the right road. When we are ready for a change, we seek things that will bring changes. TM was one of those things for me. It replaced some of my loneliness with solitude. But it was not enough. It could make me feel less frustrated but it couldn't help me break old habits that were ruining my marriage. However, it did open my mind to other possibilities. After I had been meditating for about a year, I reached a plateau.

It was then that a friend gave me the book *Born to Win* by Muriel James and Dorothy Jongeward. I started to read it on my way home one evening on what was then known as the Ravenswood elevated train. People sometimes say a book has changed their lives. This was such a book for me. A year later or earlier, *Born to Win* would not have had the impact that it did on that winter evening in Chicago. It described transactional analysis and gestalt. It was to be my first experience in self-analysis.

Born to Win spoke to me directly, merging with the mood I was in, speaking to the very problems I was wrestling with. My marriage needed repair more desperately than ever. The book was about the way people respond to one another. It was a revelation to me. I learned that I could, in a rational way, dissect my emotions, break down my response patterns, and actually see and understand what caused them.

Shortly after I finished the book, I began transactional analysis with a therapist. TM gave me distance and perspective as far as my emotions were concerned, but transactional analysis took me one step further and gave me a formula for understanding some of my emotional cul-de-sacs. I felt a tremendous burden lift from me, and from that moment, my loneliness was never as total, or desperate, as it had been before—as it had been when I was a child who did not understand herself, her body, or her mind, and so would cry out in terror in the night.

The book describes "winners" and "losers." A winner "learns to know his feelings and his limitations and is not afraid of them. He is not stopped by his own contradictions and ambivalences. He knows when he is angry and can listen when others are angry with him. He can give and receive affection. He is able to love and be loved."

Some losers "speak of themselves as successful but anxious, successful but trapped, or successful but unhappy. Others speak of themselves as totally beaten, without purpose, unable to move, half dead, or bored to death. A loser may not recognize that, for the most part, he has been building his own cage and digging his own grave, and is a bore to himself."

On Loneliness

I wanted to be a winner but felt like a loser. I read on. I read about the psychological games that people play, games left over from childhood, and I saw that my husband and I played many of them. We lived for the future and not in the present. We blamed each other for our unhappiness. We got into fights so that we would withdraw and avoid intimacy. We would collect grudges against each other and then cash them in at the right moment. This was all done discreetly, of course. On the surface, our marriage was affectionate and unruffled, but underneath, these games were going on.

I worked for three months with this therapist and tore myself apart and slowly put myself back together piece by piece. I learned that I grew up strangled by my emotions, never saying what I really felt, always dishonest and afraid. I began clearing away some of the emotional debris from my past.

I learned to see when I was acting like my mother, when I was acting like a four-year-old child again, and when I was acting like a rational adult. For example, after a full day of work, I would often come home and prepare an elaborate meal. Usually, my husband did not help. I didn't ask him to help. I did it with a smile; it was, in fact, my idea. But I also thought it was expected of me and I resented it. I was tired from working all day and didn't feel like waiting on anyone at night. But I didn't say anything. I learned from my mother to keep a stiff upper lip, and so I suffered in silence. I remembered from my childhood that when things didn't go my way it was easiest to cry, and if that didn't work, keep quiet—so I kept quiet.

My husband, at the same time, was playing his own games. He, too, was reliving his childhood reactions. When I made a point of being silent, he withdrew—as he had done with his parents when he was growing up. Neither of us was doing what we really wanted to do, which was to get angry and blow up so that we could break out of the cage and be free to develop our relationship rather than duplicate old ones.

We both pretended to be something we weren't, believing that was how the other person wanted us to be. We manipulated each other. These games kept us from being intimate. We wore too many masks. Transactional analysis helped me see that and helped me decide the marriage had to either change or end.

There is a parable in *Born to Win* about a man who finds a young eagle, takes it home, and puts it in the barnyard where it soon begins to act as if it were a chicken. A naturalist passes by and sees the eagle. He tells the farmer it can still be taught to fly, but each time the naturalist lifts it into the air, the eagle jumps back to the ground and runs to the chicken coop.

Finally, on the third try, the eagle stretches its wings and lifts off with a trembling and triumphant cry. "It may be that the eagle still remembers the chickens with nostalgia . . . but as far as anyone knows, he has never returned to lead the life of a chicken. He was an eagle though he had been kept and tamed as a chicken." I thought about that eagle, how he must have felt that first time— the pull of his wings and the arc of his flight.

When I left the marriage, I felt like that eagle. It was comfortable to be married, safe, and secure. But for me it was unnatural; I was frightened but relieved when I felt strong enough to leave.

My early exposure to TM and transactional analysis made me curious about other circa- 1970s therapeutic groups and their leaders. So when I heard that the Indian guru, Sri Swami Satchidananda, was going to speak at the Church of St. John the Divine in Manhattan, I decided to go. I wasn't disappointed. He had a snow-white beard, long silver hair, and olive skin. His socks were orange, his robe was pale peach, and he was seated on a matching peach dais.

His eyes pierced mine from thirty feet away. He was completely unself-conscious and his laughter, which seemed to just seep out of him like water from a leaky cup, was mirthful like a child's. The message was: People are basically good and pure; we must scrape away the cruelty of society, get back to basics, learn self-control. Then we will find bliss and the peace that converts the agony of loneliness into saintly solitude.

"We do not control our ordinary senses—our eyes, nose, ears, sense of touch," Satchidananda said. "We aren't even aware of all the things in this room, and yet we want ESP, we want to know what's in the room next door. We do not control our senses; we are slaves to them! The cigarette is master over us. The things we see in the store windows; they are not there for us to use—they are there to use us." He spoke for an hour. It was impressive, dramatic, and fun. Because of that, I decided to indulge my curiosity a bit further and signed up then and there for a five-day yoga retreat in Massachusetts.

The retreat was held in a new section of a Catholic convent. For five days I walked, ate, and worked in total silence. I sat cross-legged, in semi-lotus position, and meditated with the rising sun. I did bellows breathing, alternate nostril breathing, hatha yoga exercise, and chanted "om shanti" a thousand times. The food was sparse: tea for breakfast; a lunch of rice or soup, steamed vegetables, and bread; two pieces of fruit for dinner. I didn't like it. There were 145 people, and after one day it seemed to me that all of them had soft eyes, soft faces, and soft hands. They seemed foolish. People who once overdosed on speed were now fretting over how much fruit juice a day was good for them or how often they should take an enema to purify the body. People with skinny arms and legs were fasting.

Everything was structured. There was no free time. For my karma yoga, I was told to wash windows in the convent's infirmary. I felt like I was in a meditation camp. The messages were simple and short:

Soul Searching

"Sit quietly and like yourself."

"Don't wait for happiness; happiness and peace are in you now."

We were told to not point our toes at the speaker because it was rude—my first lesson in Indian etiquette. The goal, we were told, was self-purification and a richer inner life.

No, I didn't like it at all. I sensed elitism, obsession with everything-in-its-place, an anal retentiveness. I stared silently at my mute dinner partners. I chewed my food slowly and reverently, as I was told. One evening, in mute revenge, I chomped down on my apple with loud lascivious bites. People stared. I hated them.

Just being in a convent was bad enough. Those aging nuns who tottered by on stubby, swollen legs, rosary beads clinking, put me through my own special hell. As an adolescent, the Catholic church had been a personal symbol of oppression. I had been educated by Dominican nuns, threatened by mortal sin, controlled by guilt, beaten with a ruler. Now all the old fears of my childhood days came back. I did not want to sleep at night in the antiseptic convent room I had been assigned: a single bed, green brick walls, a wash basin, one desk, and, over it, a crucifix with a silver Jesus. I woke up in the middle of the night feeling once again the terror of the child who felt she was not pure enough, holy enough, or good enough to be loved—the child who feared the flames of hell.

On the first window-washing day, I took up my bucket and rags and found that my hands were shaking. My head was split with pain, and a deep furrow ran between my eyebrows. I held my tongue; I wanted to see if I could do it or if I would be overtaken by the rage of my past. A young woman gathered us together in the infirmary. She said: "Let us learn from the nuns' example, from their lives of dedication and sacrifice." We chanted for Jesus and the Blessed Virgin Mary. I remembered the nuns from my school days, their faces red with anger, distorted with hate, shaking their fists at those of us who made mistakes when writing the Our Father in Latin.

Now, these nuns seemed like children. On each bedside table were the trinkets of their lives: plaster-of-Paris statuettes, gilt-edged holy cards, framed pictures of the Holy Family. I washed the windows silently.

The second day in the infirmary, a bedridden and half-blind nun called out to me, "Sister, please, give me a glass of water." I was wearing a dark blouse and skirt, and she thought I was a nun. I went to her, brought her water, and held her hand. She seemed so lonely, and it cost me little to pretend. I saw that they feared death just like the rest of us; they grasped and pleaded and cried in their time of dying. They scratched at death with brittle, broken nails. Their prayer books were faded, their scapulars frayed, and their pictures of favorite Cardinals curled at the edges.

While washing windows, I wondered about the other people on the retreat who seemed to thirst for prayer, ritual, and imposed controls on diet, sex, and lifestyle. Were they the children of liberal parents? Were they reactionaries against their own radicalism?

On the fourth day, Easter morning, I passed the small convent chapel on the way to breakfast tea. Through a side door, I saw an aging priest giving communion. The door was at the end of a long narrow hall leading to the chapel, and the sun spotlighted the priest and the communicants who were shuffling forward to him one by one, dressed in Easter best: the priest in white robes, little girls in pink coats, and ladies in hats. It was like looking at a slice of my past. I stopped, I stared, I longed, for an instant, to believe again. Life was so simple then, so cut and dried, and I had gone through so much confusion since. With that brief longing came other memories, and I knew I couldn't go back.

Soul Searching

On the final day, I woke up in my convent room feeling as if a fever had broken—an emotional fever. I felt wonderful. I didn't mind washing their windows anymore. The battle was over. I didn't have to run anymore. I didn't fear them anymore. I don't know exactly how it happened, but I went through a tunnel and came out the other end. It broke down a major barrier for me, one that had kept me lonely most of my life. When I had believed the nuns, I felt guilty for my sins and lonely in my guilt. When I had rejected the nuns, I felt defensive about my decision and isolated from my family. But now the guilt and the defensiveness were gone.

I left the convent the next morning feeling light and pure. The meditation, meager diet, and vast expanse of silence had freed me. That unexpected confrontation had confirmed me. The yoga retreat was for me a time and place of healing. When I spoke again after five days of silence, the words seemed to come from a long distance, and I watched them form and dissipate like vapor. Most words seemed unnecessary. I had the right to remain silent. I was changed, and yet in the changing I had remained the same. I had met myself, that was all. On the bus home, I felt I had taken a long journey that went in a circle, and now I was back where I started. I saw who I had been, and for the first time, I was not afraid.

Once, just once, I have heard people let loose of their repressed emotions, and I found it terrifying. It happened during a "process" in est, which closed in 1984, thank God. I found out about est by accident when I discovered a seminar was being held in a hotel where I was attending a meeting. I was surprised to find that est had reached the East Coast; I'd always thought of it as a California phenomenon. I had been thinking of writing an article on the group, and here was my chance to begin researching.

The est training involved sitting in a hotel conference room for two weekends and being deluged with a combination of

153

gestalt, Zen, group therapy, Scientology, and Esalen techniques—
with a dose of brainwashing thrown in for effect.

During this process, two hundred people, myself included,
were told to lie on the floor and close our eyes and pretend we
were afraid of the person next to us; then the next four people
closest to us; then all the people in the hotel; in the city; and in the
country. Moans and cries rose from the room, and soon lawyers
and doctors and artists and secretaries were writhing and screaming on the floor. This is called the "fear process." I heard them and
began to be afraid of their fear, heard myself moaning, "No, no,"
and felt tears on my cheeks. Nothing wraps us in isolation more
surely than the fear of other people, and nothing is more frightening than to have this fear released en masse.

Most of the people seemed to be there because they were
afraid of other things as well: afraid of failure; of success; of infe-
riority; of their husbands or parents; afraid of loving, or being
unloved. I don't know how indicative they were of the average
population but by the end of the second weekend, the frustration
and desperation of these people, myself included, made us stand
up and tell all about ourselves: our infidelities, our nightmares,
our phobias. It was a catharsis, as if emotional constipation had at
last been relieved. We let it all go.

During another process, we were asked to close our eyes and
bring to mind whatever in our life bothered us most. I thought
of my loneliness—the abstract concept, the pain that filtered
through my life. Then the trainer told us to give whatever we were
thinking of a physical form.

Behind my closed eyelids I saw a bright white stage. At center stage sat a small humped person on a stool, legs drawn up
in a fetal position. I watched the figure from the rear of a dark
and empty auditorium. When it sensed my presence, it slowly
lifted the top half of its body, like a jackknife unfolding, raised

its wrinkled face, and opened its mouth, wider and wider until it was a black hole.

When it began to wail, the sound was a single note, round and resonant from the back of its throat. It was like the sound I imagine coming from Munch's "The Scream." It rolled over me like waves and sucked at me like an undertow.

I reached out my arms to comfort the crumpled figure and realized I was reaching out to embrace my own loneliness. I recoiled in horror, for that was me up there on the stage. It was the ugly, best-forgotten part of me.

Slowly, I lowered my arms. I felt numb. In this vision I turned and left the auditorium, locking the door behind me. I opened my eyes, and the scene disappeared. My confusion and terror seemed silly. I had "seen" my loneliness, but had been unable to confront or destroy it. I was left with a fascinating, but useless, image. What had I just gone through?

What I had gone through was a type of self-hypnosis; est wore us down emotionally and intellectually. We had little food, sleep, or time to go to the bathroom. By evening, when most of these self-confrontation techniques took place, we had been sitting in our chairs for about twelve hours. The revelations came when we were most susceptible: when we were tired, numb, and vulnerable.

Erich Fromm, when talking about the psychology of Nazism, described similar techniques that were used by Hitler. He points out that, in *Mein Kampf,* Hitler wrote: "In the morning and even during the day, men's willpower revolts with highest energy against an attempt at being forced under another's will. In the evening, however, they succumb more easily to the dominating force of a stronger will."

Once resistance is low, weakened by a hard day at work, or, as in the case of est, by physical discomfort, we are more easily converted to the cause, whatever that cause may be. Fromm says the conditions that made people ready to submit to the Nazis were present then (and certainly remain present today). He calls them: "a state of inner tiredness and resignation, which is characteristic of the individual in the present era even in democratic countries." Hitler advocated large gatherings (as did est) as the most effective way to sway people, who succumb easily "to the magic influence of what we call mass suggestion."

I don't know if Werner Erhard, the founder of est, realized this when he outlined his program. But the resemblance made me uncomfortable, especially because the techniques work so well. It also didn't help me to know that Werner Erhard's real name was Jack Rosenberg and that he had changed it to one with a more Aryan ring.

From the beginning of the est training, when it was made clear to all of us that it was a "safe space" in which we could vent our pain, grief, and sadness, it reminded me of Gunter Grass's "safe space" in his book *The Tin Drum,* and his description of the Onion Cellar—a place of entertainment in post-World War II Germany. It was very special. There was no music, food, or liquor. Each evening, people would sit at bare tables, waiting. On cue, the owner of the Onion Cellar would pass out cutting boards in the shape of pigs or fish along with paring knives and onions. On his signal, everyone peeled their onions and as they peeled they began to cry. As they cried, they opened up and talked about themselves. The onion juices "did what the world and the sorrows of the world could not do: it brought forth a round, human tear. It made them cry. At last they were able to cry again. To cry properly, without restraint, to cry like mad. The tears flowed and washed everything away. The rain came. The dew . . . human beings who have had a good cry open their mouths to speak. Still hesitant, startled by the nakedness of their own words, the weepers poured out their hearts to their neighbors . . . and submitted to questioning, let themselves be turned inside-out like overcoats."

In many ways some—perhaps most—of us Americans suffer from the same illnesses. We have retreated into ourselves. We trust nothing and no one so, afraid of yet another betrayal, we find spaces and ways in which to vent: It could be a good scream in a car with windows rolled up, or a marathon workout. In our culture, especially, it could turn to rage: violent acts in places where people can't fight back—schools, places of worship—a murderous scream into the world.

An experience like est leaves many people feeling high, at least for a month or two. Certainly life seemed less upsetting to me. I accepted a lot of small, daily things that used to frustrate me. Before, if I lost my house keys, I would be angry and upset. Life seemed so difficult. Now, I saw that I did it to myself; I accepted responsibility for my stupidities. It became easier for me to say no, be honest, be less demanding; est brought life back down to basics. It was a good hype, but dangerous for some and in the long run not effective for me.

By this time, I'd had my fill of popular disciplines, and when a chance came along to participate in Arica, a movement that tries to unify mind, body, and emotions to make us feel whole again—I passed. In Arica, as in many of these groups, emotions like loneliness and sadness are lower states of consciousness, oriented towards death rather than life. Once you reach higher states of consciousness, you will be neither lonely nor happy, just flowing. You will not be "in contradiction with the energy of the planet," said Oscar Ichazo, founder of Arica. Like most others, its leaders claim it can lead us to these higher states, can help us break out of our uptight habits, can dissolve our egos. Once we have done that, loneliness is no longer significant. Then we just feel, in Maslow's words, "individuality freed of isolation." In Arica, you hold hands, look in one another's eyes, share the things you most fear, tell each other what you truly think and feel about them. It was not for me, especially after est.

All these popular disciplines, it seems to me, are telling us the same things: that we have the right to celebrate our unique inner core without letting that uniqueness shut us off from others; that we can acknowledge our specialness and our need for other people; that we share a common fate. These groups show us how to open up, drop defenses, how to be with people without distrust or resentment. They show us how to look openly in others' eyes without flashing messages or building walls. They teach us how to play again.

The Bible says that unless we become again as little children, we shall not enter into the kingdom of Heaven. These groups express the same sentiment. The differences are that today Heaven is called nirvana or cosmic consciousness, there are many ways of getting there, and the alternative isn't necessarily Hell— just something less than Heaven.

Because people are free to use these groups in whatever way they need, some have used them to promote a new narcissism based not on how big a house you have but on how enlightened you are. An example of this happened to me in my optometrist's office. A young man smiled at me as I walked in. I smiled back and picked up a magazine. When I looked up a few minutes later, he was still smiling at me in the same way. I smiled back, a little uneasily. Five minutes later when I looked up again, he was still smiling with the same fixed grin. I asked him why he was smiling. "I'm a Scientologist," he said. "I keep getting higher and higher without drugs. I can't stop smiling. Sometimes I get cramps in the back of my neck from smiling so much."

Of the many paths I have taken, none has been slower, more painful, or more useful than private therapy with a person you can trust who you can allow to become a tutor/parent/friend/antagonist—a person who interacts with you in a warm and reassuring way. I grew up in an environment where you went into therapy only if you were flipping off the walls. It was, I thought, absurd to pay someone money just to listen to you. I mean, what are friends for? For these reasons, and because I was broke, I waited far too long. I finally called a therapist when I realized that popular movements, such as TM, transactional analysis, yoga, est, and Arica, only helped me in a limited way.

All these groups focused on my problems and helped me solve some. But none was equipped, I found out, to get down to the basic, deep-rooted causes of my loneliness and alienation.

I spent my first few sessions with the therapist crying about how lonely and miserable I was. Finally, she told me my tears were boring, and we got down to business. Gradually, I saw my own particular problems, my own particular reasons for keeping people at arm's length. I began to realize I had never been able to separate myself from my mother; I started to understand why I had never acted maturely with men. I saw how I was fossilized in my childhood, had stayed so embedded in my past that the present often flowed by without touching or affecting me.

Slowly and painfully I tried (and am trying) to extricate myself. In conjunction with private therapy, I was advised to join a group therapy session once a week. Other people in the group helped me recognize when my reactions were inappropriate, when I became defensive, how I lied in subtle ways. Through therapy, I understand that I have needs that can never be filled, needs that come out of an old emptiness that has no relation to what is really going on around me.

Now that I understand and have resolved most of the deepest problems I took with me into therapy, I stay on for other, more exciting reasons: to see the broader sweep of things; live with less pain; to unburden myself of the universal shame that seems to infest all of us; to peel off layers of myself like those desperate people in the Onion Cellar peeled away their onion skins; to become more honest and clear about who I am so that, by the time of my dying, I am back to where I began, without falseness or pretense, without duplicity, with much curiosity, and only a trace of fear.

❦ 11

Freedom

"Where there is loneliness there is also sensitivity,
and where there is sensitivity there is awareness
and recognition and promise."
(Clark Moustakas, Loneliness)

For years, I refused to look at my loneliness. Instead of facing it, I fought it off. I won some battles but lost many more. When I finally learned to accept my loneliness rather than struggle against it, it disappeared. When I stopped running from it, it stopped pursuing me. It seems strange, now, to have learned something simple in such a hard way.

Many of the problems and much of the pain I felt came from trying to resist my loneliness. The moment we begin to build a wall against it, we have already lost. If we can't acknowledge it and go with it, it ends up controlling us. Before we can look at our loneliness, we must stop trying to resist it. We must stop blaming romantic partners, children, or bosses for our feelings of loneliness and alienation in our lives. We must accept total responsibility for who we are.

We are full of conflicts, and to try to eliminate them is to alienate us from ourselves. It creates empty feelings in us. Instead of fighting them, we must learn to live with our contradictions and to value them, or, as Erikson said, we must "have the courage of our diversity." We must learn, often contrary to what we have been taught in school, that it is okay to be many people, okay to change your mind, okay to feel one way today and a different way tomorrow, okay to be wrong.

One effect of the drug LSD is that people lose their social veneer and their egos seem to disintegrate into the many personalities that are already there. They sense the fragmented parts of themselves. Some say they seem to "die" psychologically and are then "reborn"—or become whole again.

While on LSD, playwright Peter Shaffer "went back" to the Bronze Age, and in his mind visited China and the Congo. He later said: "I have never forgotten it or moved far from the sense of wonder it provided and a fairly constant gratitude for the infinite complexity of being it revealed to me. It also abolished forever any lingering sense of guilt in me about containing so many contradictory selves."

Through the drugs he took, Carlos Castenada became "a thousand pieces at once . . . I exploded . . . it released something I had kept locked up all my life . . . there was no longer the sweet unity I call 'me.' I was a myriad of selves which were all 'me,' a colony of separate units that had a special allegiance to one another and would join unavoidably to form one single awareness, my human awareness . . . this was my life force . . ."

We all are capable of feeling the multiple parts of ourselves, experiencing ourselves fully without drugs or other props. All we have to do is be with ourselves. If this sounds like armchair existentialism, something so obvious it doesn't even have to be put into words, that is because it *is* very obvious. We already know this; we just act as if we don't.

Watch people on the street sometime. Notice how most of

them do not seem to be with themselves. Some seem lost in thought—they are at last night's party, at tomorrow's meeting, or already thinking of dinner. Or they are self-conscious, so wrapped up in how they appear to other people that they no longer have any sense of who they really are, of what they mean to themselves.

How often I have watched people in restaurants watching themselves in the mirrors of other people's eyes, as if the reflection of themselves through others is the only way they can assure themselves they exist. Some of the best actors and actresses have commented on how often people in real life seem to be acting a part rather than really living.

You know when a person is absorbing life every second: She or he is magnetic, dynamic, has a force that we envy. We wonder how they got to be that way.

Marlon Brando was one of these people. A friend said of him: "When Brando stands still, he is mysteriously surrounded by his own space . . . Offstage he may suddenly disconcert by non-sequiturs and interruptions: 'Why do you look down into your whisky, why don't you look around the color of it?' . . . Or he might be fascinated by your thumbs or the opening and shutting of a purse . . . observing, always capturing some small importance and releasing it like a bird from his hand. "

Bob Dylan often gives the impression of having this tunnel vision, this ability to immerse himself in the details and small flashes of life. "Dylan electrifies [an audience] by polarizing it," wrote Joan Didion in the *Woodstock Times*. "I am I, and you are you, he says in no uncertain terms . . . His presence is built of the courage to stand alone and the intensity with which he stands guard at his own gate. He does not reject himself, he is whole. He is all there, implying that relations would be charged with energy. He would look in your eye and burn a hole in your brain."

On Loneliness

When we are near people who have a unity, a certainty, a flow to their lives, it makes us feel peaceful. The mime artist Marcel Marceau had that effect on me. He captures each second as if on film, frame by frame, and then he feeds it back. The past turns into the present with the precision of a snap of the finger. Each movement, each gesture, so clearly recalled that it washes over me like a poem. My life—all life—is crystallized. Mime, says Marceau, is silent music for the soul.

All of us have this ability to be aware, spontaneous, open. As Buddhist teacher, author, and American nun Pema Chodron puts it, "We all have moments of appreciating what we see or taste or smell—just as it is. We relax and out of nowhere we accept our experience without wanting anything to be more or less or different. We feel that everything, at least for the moment, is complete. When our mind is open and fresh, we see beauty everywhere, including within ourselves . . . We're in tune with the transience of the world, with its poignancy and its profound richness."

We begin to live stunted lives when we repress emotions like loneliness, sadness, mourning, and anger—when we act the way we think we should act instead of just relaxing into who we really are.

We learn as infants to express only certain feelings and hide the rest. Our parents and teachers tell us to behave, be quiet, be friendly, be cheerful. We become socialized. This repression is why, even if we are outgoing, successful, happily married, and have many friends, we may feel it is all happening *to* us and not *in* us, and this is why some people go through their entire lives as if they are swimming in a wet suit instead of their flesh, and the water never touches them.

It is why they jump from windows instead of looking out of them. At the bottom of our yearning is our despair. Very few of us know how to live with this despair, which is why we have become a nation with "skyrocketing rates of suicide and overdose deaths."

Unfortunately, some people think even now that it is a sign of weakness, a stigma, to admit despair or self-doubt, to become unsure of your life, allow yourself to break down emotionally. This isn't necessarily so. People who live fully know their pain and do not fear it. Abraham Lincoln suffered from massive depression all his life and so did Winston Churchill, who said that "depression is my lap dog." People who run away from their despair, who are afraid to suffer, find this fear can deaden them and dominate their lives. "When you are trying to avoid suffering, and you are afraid of death, your whole philosophy in life is built on the fear of suffering and the fear of death," Ram Dass writes in *The Only Dance There Is.*

It seems inevitable that certain life experiences will lead to pain. Every time we take a chance, we become vulnerable. It is like learning to walk all over again. As we move forward, we experience a second of being off-balance, a hesitation, the chance of falling. But, as children, the moment we fell we got up and started walking again. Life remains like that: We are on-balance, off-balance, we move forward, fall down, get up, and start over.

I watched a friend of mine going through a nervous breakdown. For weeks she moved through the world as if she had a veil over her face, and she saw everything through a black film of pain. She heard people speaking, saw their lips move, but could not remember what they said. She felt that her emotions were on ice. She was fired from her job and her lover left. In her confusion and fright, she fled alone to Europe. I took her to the airport.

She wrote to me from a small hotel in Madrid where she was staying alone. "I am no longer afraid of death," she wrote. "I have dreams that a wall of fog rolls in at night to smother me, but the dreams don't frighten me anymore."

She stayed alone in the hotel for several weeks and then moved in with a man she had just met. "We don't talk about the future," she wrote. "It's enough to give and get some comfort in the night."

Through all this, she slowly began to heal. "I feel the core solidify in me again," she wrote. "I find great joy in holding a clean earthen cup, touching a polished table. I identify with solid, simple things. I move gingerly, as if I'm recuperating from a fever."

When she returned, I noticed a change in her. She was more sure of herself, less polite, and more honest. She had come through her despair, she said. It had been like a death; she had touched an icy core inside. Now she knew, having faced it, that she would not crack.

I have also gone through periods of despair over my limitations, including the time I've wasted, the mistakes I've made, fallen hopes, and broken dreams. Each time, my deep and isolating pain has been followed by a joy of release.

Hermann Hesse writes: "Every occasion when a mask was torn off, an ideal broken, was preceded by this hateful vacancy and stillness, this deathly constriction and loneliness and unrelatedness, this waste and empty hell of lovelessness and despair . . ." This was certainly true for me.

But to have value, such an experience must be more than self-indulgence or masochism. It must be productive. It must reveal the deeper regions of our existence. Anne Morrow Lindbergh explained: "If suffering alone taught, all the world would be wise, since everyone suffers. To suffering must be added mourning, understanding, patience, love, openness, and the willingness to remain vulnerable."

Such experiences can be frightening if we are not ready for them. It can be horrifying to tear ourselves apart and see what is underneath. But when it is over, it will seem so simple that we will want to laugh at the half-remembered pain. The pain will still be there but it won't control us once we have dealt with it. "Despair is the only cure for illusion . . . a kind of mourning period for our fantasies. Some people do not survive this despair, but no major change within a person can occur without it," says Slater. In the long run, it is much more destructive to deny it or ignore that entire part of ourselves than it is to run the gauntlet. Until we take that step, we remain prisoners of our past in a fortress of our own making.

Most of us live sedentary, cautious lives, and the resulting flab afflicts the mind as well as the body. We settle for security, for a comfortable, glossy surface to our lives. We constrict our lives to make them manageable when our lives should be ever-expanding like helium balloons, rising higher and higher into air so thin it leaves us gasping, dazzled, and awestruck.

Most of us, however, choose not to take chances and settle instead for khaki-colored loneliness—dulled familiarity and quiet discontent. This is the loneliness of sitting night after night in front of our various screens connecting through bytes, bits, and other digital units of measure, being tolerable, reasonable, and afraid of just about everything.

These are the small towns of our minds. In the town where I grew up, it was not the dull Sundays that bothered me, or endless cruising in borrowed cars, or drinking beer in long dark bars. It was, rather, the attitude toward it all: the joylessness and inevitability of it. That is what I fled. I tried to outdistance it so I would not be sucked into a life that smothered me, limited me, and threatened my growth. I believed that if I stayed, my life would be lukewarm, a castoff of my dreams.

It was hard to break away. I had to be analyzed and hurt and do a lot of hurting myself. I had to shatter the dreams people had about me, and then have my dreams shattered in turn. As Doris Lessing says: "How did marvelous, mature, wise people get to be that way? Well, we know, don't we? Every bloody one of them's got a history of emotional crime, oh, the sad bleeding corpses that litter the road to maturity of the wise, serene man or woman of fifty-odd."

I, for one, would not want to go home again.

"To live," says Octavio Paz, "is to be separated from what we were in order to approach what we are going to be in the mysterious future. . . . Man is the only being who knows he is alone . . . His nature . . . consists in his longing to realize himself in another. Man is nostalgia and a search for communion . . ."

A child's growth is a constant pull away from the familiar toward the unknown, a continual rending asunder, a cycle of loneliness. Growth brings conflict and loneliness. We want to be free and belong; we want to be alone and we want to be with people. When we say that we "don't know what we want," it is usually because we want it all. What we don't know, too often, is that we can have it all, find joy in it all, but it takes a lot of work and energy and courage.

It took me a while to recognize that loneliness per se is neither good nor bad. True, it is almost always painful. Yes, it makes us suffer, but it also makes us whole. It is a natural extension of loving and caring, of deep involvement with other people. Loneliness is what happens when we feel close to someone and then pull away. This is one reason why some of us cry, or want to cry, after having sex with someone we love. That pain of pulling apart, of feeling separate again, is a normal reaction to love. The law of physical response applies, in this case, to emotional response as well: For every action, there is an equal and opposite reaction. If we feel close at times, then we are also going to feel separate at other times. If in our closeness we expose our vulnerabilities to another person, then we are going to feel all the more threatened by separation. When we share our love, we share our anxieties.

Freedom

This is part of the duality of living: love and hate, joy and pain, loneliness and intimacy. Ram Dass says of life: "It's all suffering: birth has in it suffering, death has in it suffering, old age has in it suffering, and sickness has in it suffering. Not getting what you want has in it suffering; getting what you don't want has in it suffering."

What he means is that pain is a corollary of our desires. Loneliness is the shadow of the needs and fears that make us love in the first place. Life is change, and the nature of change is loneliness.

Change isn't always dramatic. It can come when we simply "forget" about ourselves, when we stop resisting and are completely receptive to something new. The moments that change us or provide new insight are most often those private moments when we literally "lose control" of ourselves and perceive something in a new way.

Writer Annie Dillard recalls in *Pilgrim at Tinker Creek* that her life was changed one afternoon when she saw an old cedar tree in a new way. "One day I was walking along Tinker Creek thinking of nothing at all and I saw the tree with the lights in it. I saw the backyard cedar where the mourning doves roost charged and transfigured, each cell buzzing with flame. I stood on the grass with the lights in it, grass that was wholly fire, utterly focused and utterly dreamed. It was less like seeing than like being for the first time seen, knocked breathless by a powerful glance. I had been my whole life a bell, and never knew it until at that moment I was lifted and struck."

Otto Friedrich describes this process in his book, *Going Crazy: Inquiry into Madness in Our Time,* as a form of temporary "insanity;" He says that it happens to all of us from time to time. It is a "breakdown in the rational mind's ability to receive and combine perceptions and to make judgments from them. And a sense of helplessness, together with a perfectly clear vision of one's own helplessness, and panic . . . it is, in some ways, like the chaotic world that we inhabit in our dreams, for there, night after night, we all go mad."

Most of us have such intense or "mystical" experiences at some point, though we may not always recognize them for what they are. One man said he has had them during orgasm. Another said he had one when he thought he was dying from injuries he received in an automobile accident. One woman, while falling asleep, saw in her mind's eye a flat octagonal wafer floating peacefully toward deep dark space. She knew it was her soul and felt an invitation to exchange the turmoil of life for the bliss of death, a tempting invitation that she declined.

I had such an experience one night in the Sinai, watching the mountains turn dark shades of purple and gray, enjoying the silence. When the sun began to rise, it was orange, as if burning from the core. Its intensity took me by surprise. I felt as if the sun, and the desert, were absorbing me, sucking me out of myself.

I felt like a swimmer dashed by strong waves against rocks, dying and yet still appreciating the power and beauty of my death. I sat unmoving. I entered a time warp and there was no distance between two thousand years ago and now. When the sun rose full it was as if a weight was lifted off me . . . as if gravity had stopped pulling at my body and I lost the sense of my Self, my ego, or whatever the nervous energy was that had been inside me. I don't know how long it lasted—I felt when it was over that I had been in a trance. I went back to my hotel and slept like a baby.

This experience in the desert along with another later in New York brought a feeling that Freud describes as "oceanic," a flood of joy and peace, of ecstasy. It went beyond loneliness, to a place where the pain of my uniqueness and isolation no longer had significance.

Freedom

Loneliness can be our teacher. It can be productive, can provide a kind of purity and power felt by some of the world's most inspiring people. Few felt the inspiration of isolation as did Thoreau or the Catholic mystic Thomas Merton. But most great people, when I think back on what I know of them, valued quiet lives. The people I most admire from history and who shaped my thoughts were loners: people like Gandhi, Simone de Beauvoir, Lincoln.

This description of the philosopher Nietzsche could probably describe other great "thinkers" of the past century: "Carefully [Nietzsche] sits down to a table; carefully the man with the sensitive stomach considers every item on the menu: no glass of wine, no glass of beer, no alcohol, no coffee, no cigar and no cigarette after his meal, nothing that stimulates, refreshes or rests him: only the short meager meal and a little urbane, unprofound conversation in a soft voice with an occasional neighbor . . . and up again into the small, narrow, modest, coldly furnished [room] . . . with no flower, no decoration, scarcely a book and rarely a letter . . . the empty silence of this strange room in which he never rests except in brief and artificially conquered sleep. Wrapped in his overcoat and a woolen scarf . . . his fingers freezing, his double glasses pressed close to the paper . . . for hours he sits like this and writes until his eyes burn."

Nietzsche himself described his loneliness as a "lonesomeness, which, as on very high mountains, often made it hard for me to breathe and made my blood rush o u t . . . ." To be different is to be for the most part alone, and sometimes lonely.

Artists—painters, writers, musicians—often learn to turn their loneliness to their advantage. They have, as Kierkegaard says, "the opportunity to become important with their despair." Out of their pain comes enlightenment; out of their agony comes inspiration. When loneliness becomes destructive or debilitating, as it did for Vincent Van Gogh and Sylvia Plath, it is because one

171

does not know how to work through it and instead lets it take over their lives.

But if we can learn from it, guide and control it, we can convert it into something positive: solitude. Gurus usually go to the desert or mountain wildernesses for solitude. Many Westerners seek it through meditation techniques. Some religious people can find it through prayer; some nature lovers can find it beside a stream. But anyone can find it; we all have the tools.

It just takes a willingness to rest in a quiet place and face ourselves. Once we give up the attachments and crutches that we think we must have in order to survive, then we begin to find out who we really are. Solitude is a time when we can transcend our daily worries, a positive time, a time for reflection and integration. All people can benefit from it.

One doctor, usually busy with hospital rounds and patients, travels alone to find solitude: "I've walked in Greece and Italy and on the wharves of LeHavre, France, by myself, and I always feel overwhelmed," he says. "I feel the kind of loneliness that adds a third dimension to my life. I suddenly realize I'm just one guy walking on this globe in this universe; it gives me a perspective on myself. When I have no ties, no appointments, when I walk for days in silence, I feel something that must be similar to what the astronauts feel in space, or what passengers feel on the deck of an ocean liner at dawn. I am small in time and space and life, and suddenly I am more precious to myself."

Solitude usually includes a time of silence. Buckminster Fuller kept almost complete silence for two years while searching for a new perspective on language. Thomas Merton said that silence actually helps us hear ourselves better. "Words stand between silence and silence: between the silence of things and the silence of our being. It is not speaking that breaks our silence, but the anxiety to be heard. If life is poured out in useless words, we will never hear anything, will never become anything, and in the end, because we have said everything before we had anything to say, we shall be left speechless at the moment of our greatest decision."

Silence gives us a chance to hear what Hermann Hesse calls "the whispering of our own blood." Solitude gives us a new kind of freedom. There are, however, many kinds of "freedom," and not all of them make us feel good.

Do we really want to be "free" from our parents, childhoods, religious beliefs, or prejudices? Do we want to be "free" from ritual, continuity, or union? I think it frightens us. I know it frightens me. Fromm says that when a person is "free from all bonds that once gave meaning and security to life . . . he cannot bear this isolation . . . he is utterly helpless in comparison with the world outside and therefore deeply afraid of it."

Freedom from loneliness is not liberation from lovers, parents, or other people, but rather liberation from ourselves from the inside out. It takes us beyond independence, to a point where our aloneness and uniqueness can be cherished and appreciated but, at the same time, our need for human contact is fulfilled.

It involves the ability to tear down defenses so we can really see ourselves and still be unafraid. It includes the willingness to be silent and sit alone. Such freedom does not come easily. It comes with hard, painful work on our emotional patterns and relationships. It comes with self-awareness and a sense of identity that goes beyond what you do for a living, where you live, or what you wear.

It is internal unity, a sense of being complete, a healthy wholeness, being in touch with our entire range of emotions, and able to express all of them without fear. This kind of freedom brings "joy, efficiency, and abandon in the face of any odds," Don Juan tells Carlos Castaneda. "That is the last lesson. It is always left for the very last moment, for the moment of ultimate solitude when a man faces his death and his aloneness. Only then does it make sense."

To be free, we must begin by accepting ourselves as we are. It is futile to pursue the illusion that something or someone outside ourselves will complete us. The illusions are why, when I am not in love, I become nostalgic for it, and why, when I am in love, I end up disappointed that the love is not as perfect as I had hoped.

The myth is that I can lose myself in someone else through love (and I can, for a moment). But, over the long haul, the love gets lost in me.

All we need for fulfillment is already in us, waiting. If we can learn to accept our own integrity, then we can begin to take pleasure in the small things of our lives. We can stop living in anticipation or retrospect and begin living in the moment. Instead of avoiding work, we can take pleasure in the work itself.

A woman from Bowling Green, Ohio, wrote to me about her own personal search for self-acceptance. For a long time, she had wished to be someone else. "I have led an average, predictable life. How difficult it was to accept myself when I realized I lacked outstanding talent . . . I fought against it, believing that the only worthy people were those who contributed something to their fellow men. I felt utter frustration when I sang and my daughter would look at me, shaking her head, and say: 'Oh, Mom' (It was that bad). Frustration when I sat down to write the great American novel, and only trivia would reveal itself. Frustration that I could not write poetry like Edna St. Vincent Millay or paint like Van Gogh."

But gradually this woman's attitude about herself changed. She decided to enjoy herself for who she was. "I did possess talent, like every human being, but my talent was not outstanding. It was a quiet, precious gift of being able to do many small things well. I began to appreciate being me. Me was OK. Ordinary can be beautiful too. I am a fine, unique person, who just never truly appreciated the beauty of her own individuality."

I know people who are lonely because they are bored, and they are bored because they do not value their own experience of living. They do not think enough of themselves to find a book they would like to read, ride a bicycle along some unexplored country road, play tennis, or learn rock-climbing or knitting or the solar system. It is true that some people use activities to avoid their loneliness, but there is also great value in being active, interested, and open.

The least lonely people I have met have a healthy balance of the two kinds of stimulation: internal and external. They are not recluses, but neither do they have to do something outside of their homes every evening. And the least lonely people I know realize they don't always have to do things with someone else to enjoy themselves: They often prefer to window-shop, see a film, or take a walk alone.

For a long time, I could not accept myself. I did not like my family and I did not like my friends. When I felt lonely, I did busy work, found a new lover, or traveled. One day I took a look at what was happening to my life and saw that nothing was happening. I saw how I had let myself be bombarded with trivia, how I had filled my days with useless details that smothered boredom but did not kill it, that let it lie there unnoticed, its flame licking away at my energy.

I began to spend a lot of time doing nothing. I began a struggle to end my isolation from myself.

"Once, in a dry season, I wrote in large letters across two pages of a notebook that innocence ends when one is stripped of the delusion that one likes oneself . . . Without [self-respect] one eventually discovers the final turn of the screw: one runs away to find oneself, and finds no one at home," Didion wrote in *Slouching*

On Loneliness

Towards Bethlehem. For the first time in my life, I sat quietly and let my demons crawl to the surface.

I began to learn the tremendous healing value of doing nothing. I learned the difference between dull days of inner emptiness and quiet days of inner peace. I spent a lot of time living without melodrama, without plans, without expectations great or small. I bought red apples and put them on a white plate, and for hours watched clouds reflected in water. I enjoyed the yawn and stretch of a cat, the swing of my hips when I kicked off my heels and walked in sneakers. Sun through stained glass. A white candle burning. I listened to music carefully and quietly without distraction.

Of course, I sometimes had to make excuses to other people and tell them I was doing something (reading, writing). But in truth, I was hibernating, recuperating from an illness that began and spread unchecked over the years. I was able, in this way, to invest all my energy in living one day whole and round. I recall those days as the most embattled, yet the most serene, of my life.

I found that a certain part of my brain was more active than ever before, that by external quietness I permitted hidden fears to rise closer to the surface. In my dreams, I was usually impotent, unable to act, or lost and trying to find my way home. I suddenly remembered past conversations, old lies, unnecessary indiscretions—after I finally gave the Being that was also me, below the surface, a little breathing room.

I stopped buying things to make me feel more beautiful and less lonely because of course they never worked for long. I found I could enjoy things without possessing them. I stopped avoiding unwanted telephone calls and confrontations, stopped being "fake nice" to people whom I stopped liking long ago. When I was worried, I would force myself to sit on my bed and think about it rather than bury it. I got angry at a lover and slammed the door in his face—angry for once, instead of just hurt.

Freedom

Before, I had tried so hard to be happy and was always disappointed. When I looked for happiness, it eluded me. When I stopped looking, it found me. Happiness, I found, is like my cat: I call and call and she will not come. But when I turn away, she suddenly leaps to my lap, purring.

Now, I feel for the first time that I am centered in my universe. The feeling comes and goes. It is a slow process, unlearning all the old taboos that isolated me in my loneliness, and I go two steps forward and one step back. But I know the only thing that counts is my experience of myself. I create the world through the way I perceive it and experience it: I can choose my life.

It does not mean that I have become indifferent. Indifference implies that a person is closed to what is happening around them. Quite the opposite has happened: I became more open. I am simply more aware of my separateness, and the things that used to threaten me no longer seem so overwhelming.

I am open to the world around me, where I once was closed. I find joy in stepping out into the world again—in seeing the face of a child, feeling the air, the ground underfoot. On paper, I structure life. I reorder it and put it into a form that makes sense for me. I twist and turn down every sentence as down an unfamiliar street. I wind into myself. Then I unwind into the chaos around me.

Outside my door, I am engulfed by color, noise, smell. The delivery boy bicycles behind his silver delivery cart; a car door slams; the corner deli sells pink roses in green tissue; fruit sits cheerily on open-air stands, sunny oranges next to sedate avocados, dusty grapes, rough melons. The sights and sounds and smells slam against me and slide off like rain from a slicker. It is a leap of faith to turn from my intricate inner world into this explosion outside my door. To write and then go back to the street is to contract and then expand. When I write, I empty like a bellows, condensing to produce a spark, and when I walk down the street

177

I fill again, slowly. When I go into the world this way, openly and with wonder, then, in that moment of solitary awareness, I begin to feel peace.

A friend called me one day from Chicago. "You make love too complicated," she said. "You try to find too much of the truth behind it. You make it dangerous because safety bores you. You are more bold, more daring than I will ever be. But tell me, in all your searching for love, what did you learn?"

I will tell my friend, when I see her again, that I have learned to live with fragility and contradiction; to survive the panic of being alone, the trauma of being unique, the pain of being alive. I have learned to recognize the need to touch another person. I have learned that change is comforting, freedom is frightening, and, in the end, the only familiar face is loneliness.

I am my own experiment.

I go on from here.

Permissions

G rateful acknowledgment is made to the following for permission to quote from copyrighted material:

Excerpts from "Little Gidding" in *Four Quartets* by T.S. Eliot. Copyright © 1936 by Houghton Mifflin Harcourt Publishing Company, renewed 1964 by T.S. Eliot. Copyright © 1940, 1941, 1942 by T.S. Eliot, renewed 1968, 1969, 1970 by Esme Valerie Eliot. Used by permission of HarperCollins Publisher.

Excerpts from my interview with William Sadler, Jr. on the taboos of admitting to loneliness. Used by permission of William Sadler, Jr.

Excerpts from my interview with Estelle Ramey on the difference between sex and love. Used by permission of Drucilla Ramey.

Excerpts from my interview with Ari Kiev on the risk of losing ourselves in love. Used by permission of Marshall Kiev.

"Daddy" from *The Collected Poems of Sylvia Plath*. Copyright © 1960, 1965, 1971, 1981 by the Estate of Sylvia Plath. Used by permission of HarperCollins Publishers.

Selection from "Romantic Towers," by Jim Reed. Used by permission of Jim Reed.

Excerpt from essay by Joan Didion in *The Woodstock Times*. Used by permission of Geddy Sveikaukas, Publisher, *The Woodstock Times*.

On Loneliness

Excerpts from *The Labyrinth of Solitude,* by Octavio Paz, reprinted courtesy of Grove Atlantic.

Excerpts from *Escape From Freedom* by Erich Fromm, on the conflict between our need for dependence and our drive to be free. Used by permission of Rainer Funk, Liepman Literary Agency.

Acknowledgments

I am grateful to the following people for sharing with me their personal and professional experiences of loneliness found in this book: former U.S. Senator James Abourezk; residents of Daytop Village in New York; Ted Bent; LaDonna Harris, founder and president of Americans for Indian Opportunity (AIM); Marshall Kiev; Dr. Ari Kiev, former director of the Social Psychiatry Research Institute in New York; Corinne Browne, Woodstock, New York; Mildred Klingman; Ted Bent; Arthur Leader, former associate executive director, Jewish Family Service; Annette Lieberman; Dr. Frank Mark, retired U.S. Public Health Service Officer; Dr. John Money, former professor of medical psychology and associate professor of pediatrics, Johns Hopkins University school of medicine; Drucilla S. Ramey; Dr. Estelle Ramey, endocrinologist and former professor, George Washington University; Dr. Richard C. Robertiello, founding director of the Long Island Consultation Center and the Long Island Institute for Mental Health; Dr. William A. Sadler, Jr., author of books on aging well, including *The Third Age: Navigating Life after 50* (with James Krefft), former professor of sociology and director of programs for the National Endowment for the Humanities, including *The American Pursuit of Loneliness*; Dr. Clifford Sager, pioneer in couples and family therapy, former clinical professor of psychiatry at Weill Cornell Medical Center.

Personal Thanks

TO: *The Authors Guild* staff, for their wonderful assistance and support, with a special thank you to Johnny Chinnici, Marketing and Communications coordinator; Kim Schefler in New York, mentor and cheerleader who gave me courage to begin this edition during the dark days of Covid; Kayla Kaufman copy editor par excellence who asked the good hard questions; Jane Friedman, for pointing me in the right direction; Karyn Driessen, former attorney and friend since grade school, for her editorial feedback and wisdom; Diane Detournay, Advanced Lecturer, English and Women, Gender, and Sexuality Studies, Fordham University, for sensitivity editing advice; Jim Feuerstein, co-founder of the web company Loft 2203 in San Antonio, for website assistance.

A special thanks to Brooke Warner, publisher of SheWritesPress/SparkPoint Studio in Berkeley, my project manager Lauren Wise, cover designer Tabitha Lahr and all the talented staff for bringing this book to fruition.

On a deeply personal level, thanks to those who *lived* this book long before it appeared: My women's group, called *Dialogue*—a Band of Sisters still there for each other after more than three decades; Joan Babinecz, dear friend, guidestar of our feisty book group whose members expanded my reading habits and I hope will be gentle with my book; Beth Murfee-DeConcini, kindred spirit and frequent editorial advisor; Elly Fine, who taught me to get away from my computer and smell the flowers. And Bruce W. for his constancy and love.

Finally I am grateful beyond words for my son Brian, the kindest, smartest and bravest person I know, who I hope will forgive me for the times I've failed him as a mother; and for my family in Wisconsin, who never stopped loving me even though I took the road less taken.

About the Author

Terri Laxton Brooks grew up in Reedsburg, Wisconsin, a farm town of one-square-mile surrounded by cornfields. The first in her family to go to college, she majored in journalism and French at the University of Wisconsin-Madison in the 1960s. Her first job out of college was as a Metro reporter for the *Chicago Tribune*. After four years at the *Tribune*, she moved to New York City, where she became a professor and then chair of the journalism department at NYU for nineteen years. She later served as dean of the Penn State college of communications. The author of three other nonfiction titles—*Bittersweet: Surviving and Growing from Loneliness, Women Can Wait: The Pleasures of Motherhood After 30,* and *Words' Worth: Write Well and Prosper*; Terri has also published hundreds of articles in publications including the *Chicago Tribune, The New York Times, Harper's, Redbook, Cosmopolitan, Columbia Journalism Review,* and *Writer's Digest*. She has a wonderful son who serves as a Lieutenant Commander on Destroyers in the U.S. Navy. She currently lives in New York City.

SELECTED TITLES FROM SHE WRITES PRESS

She Writes Press is an independent publishing company
founded to serve women writers everywhere.
Visit us at www.shewritespress.com.

A Delightful Little Book on Aging by Stephanie Raffelock. $19.95, 978-1-63152-840-8. A collection of thoughts and stories woven together with a fresh philosophy that helps to dispel some of the toxic stereotypes of aging, this inspirational, empowering, and emotionally honest look at life's journey is part joyful celebration and part invitation to readers to live life fully to the very end.

Falling Together: How to Find Balance, Joy, and Meaningful Change When Your Life Seems to be Falling Apart by Donna Cardillo. $16.95, 978-1-63152-077-8. A funny, big-hearted self-help memoir that tackles divorce, caregiving, burnout, major illness, fears, and low self-esteem—and explores the renewal that comes when we are able to meet these challenges with courage.

Green Nails and Other Acts of Rebellion: Life After Loss by Elaine Soloway. $16.95, 978-1-63152-919-1. An honest, often humorous account of the joys and pains of caregiving for a loved one with a debilitating illness.

Note to Self: A Seven-Step Path to Gratitude and Growth by Laurie Buchanan. $16.95, 978-1-63152-113-3. Transforming intention into action, *Note to Self* equips you to shed your baggage, bridging the gap between where you are and where you want to be—body, mind, and spirit—and empowering you to step into joy-filled living *now!*

Raw: My Journey from Anxiety to Joy by Bella Mahaya Carter. $16.95, 978-1-63152-345-8. In an effort to holistically cure her chronic stomach problems, Bella Mahaya Carter adopted a 100 percent raw, vegan diet—a first step on a quest that ultimately dragged her, kicking and screaming, into spiritual adulthood.

Tell Me Your Story: How Therapy Works to Awaken, Heal, and Set You Free by Tuya Pearl. $16.95, 978-1-63152-066-2. With the perspective of both client and healer, this book moves you through the stages of therapy, connecting body, mind, and spirit with inner wisdom to reclaim and enjoy your most authentic life.